I0003747

Angular

If you have any questions, comments, or feedback about this book, I would love to hear from you. Please feel free to reach out to me via email:

Email: ec.books.contact@gmail.com

Copyright© 2024 by Eldar Cohen

Table of Contents

Info

The code in this guide was tested on Angular 18.

There may be certain syntax, code constructs, or concepts that are not explained in some topics, but they will be discussed later to avoid confusing the reader.

This book is written in a minimalistic style and follows a logical flow of topics, allowing you to write programs quickly without unnecessary delays.

Prerequisites

JavaScript - Proficiency in the JavaScript language is a must, look for the book JavaScript by Eldar Cohen at amazon. https://www.amazon.com/dp/B0CQD3SHY4

TypeScript - Preferred, but it's not mandatory. look for the book TypeScript by Eldar Cohen at amazon. https://www.amazon.com/dp/B0CQS3JKRY

HTML - Basic html is mandatory. look for the book HTML by Eldar Cohen at amazon. https://www.amazon.com/dp/B0CNQG1HD6

CSS - Basic css is mandatory.

Single-Page Web Applications

Single-Page Web Applications (SPAs) are web applications or websites that load a single HTML page and dynamically update the content as the user interacts with the application. In traditional multi-page applications, navigating to different sections or pages typically involves reloading the entire page from the server. SPAs, on the other hand, use AJAX (Asynchronous JavaScript and XML) and other technologies to retrieve data and update the page without a full page reload.

Key characteristics and advantages of Single-Page Web Applications:

Fluid User Experience: SPAs provide a smoother and more responsive user experience because they can update content dynamically without requiring a full page reload. This approach eliminates the flicker or delay associated with traditional page transitions.

Faster Navigation: Since SPAs load all necessary resources (HTML, CSS, and JavaScript) initially and only fetch data as needed, subsequent interactions with the application are generally faster. This is especially noticeable when navigating between different sections of the application.

State Preservation: SPAs maintain the application state on the client side, reducing the need to send data back and forth between the client and server. This enables users to seamlessly continue their interactions without losing context.

Smoother Transitions: SPAs often use client-side routing to manage different views or sections of the application. This allows for smooth transitions between views without full page reloads, contributing to a more seamless user experience.

Popular JavaScript frameworks and libraries, such as Angular, React, and Vue.js, are commonly used to build SPAs. These frameworks provide tools for managing state, handling routing, and efficiently updating the DOM, making it easier for developers to create interactive and dynamic user interfaces.

Angular Introduction

Angular is an open-source web application framework developed by Google. It is written in TypeScript and enables developers to build dynamic, single-page web applications (SPAs). Angular provides a comprehensive set of tools and features for various aspects of web development.

Modular Architecture: Angular applications are constructed using a modular architecture where functionality is organized into modules. This approach enhances code organization, maintainability, and reusability.

Two-way Data Binding: Angular offers two-way data binding, implying that changes in the user interface (UI) automatically update the application state, and vice versa. This simplifies the process of managing and updating the UI.

Dependency Injection: Angular's dependency injection system makes it easy to manage and organize the components of an application. It promotes the creation of loosely coupled components, enhancing code modularity and testability.

Directives: Angular uses directives to extend HTML with new attributes and tags. Directives provide a way to create reusable components and manipulate the DOM. There are three main types of directives in Angular: Component Directives, Attribute Directives, and Structural Directives.

Services: Services in Angular are singletons that can be used to encapsulate and share functionality across different components. They are often employed to handle tasks such as data retrieval, authentication, and communication with servers.

Forms: Angular provides a form handling mechanism with two different approaches: template-driven forms and reactive forms. These mechanisms allow for the creation and validation of user input.

Routing: Angular includes a routing system that enables developers to create SPAs with multiple views and navigation between them.

Testing: Angular has built-in support for testing, making it easy to write unit tests for components, services, and other parts of the application.

Development Environment

To develop Angular applications, you'll need a code development environment, also called as Integrated Development Environment (IDE)

1. Visual Studio Code (VS Code) - lightweight, free, and open-source code editor developed by Microsoft

   https://visualstudio.microsoft.com/downloads

2. Chrome or other browsers

3. Node.js https://nodejs.org/en/download

4. TypeScript

5. Angular CLI

Useful Links

Angular docs - https://angular.io

Create Angular Project

1. Install Visual Studio Code

   https://visualstudio.microsoft.com/downloads

2. Install Node.js https://nodejs.org/en/download

3. Create apps folder C:\apps

4. Open Visual Studio Code in the folder you created

5. In VS Code Press View Tab -> Terminal

6. In the Terminal Install TypeScript - `npm i typescript`

7. In the Terminal Install Angular CLI - `npm i @angular/cli`

8. In the Terminal Create new angular app:

   `ng new EldarAngular --no-standalone`

   chose stylesheet format, I use less

```
? Which stylesheet format would you like to use?
  CSS
  SCSS    [ https://sass-lang.com/documentation/syntax#scss      ]
  Sass    [ https://sass-lang.com/documentation/syntax#the-indented-syntax ]
> Less    [ http://lesscss.org                                   ]
```

chose to enable Server-Side Rendering (SSR):

```
? Do you want to enable Server-Side Rendering (SSR) and Static Site Generation (SSG/Prerendering)? (y/N) y
```

Wait for the files to download

9. Open Visual Studio Code in the EldarAngular folder

Project Files

.vscode Folder: This folder contains Visual Studio Code-specific settings and configurations for your project.

extensions.json: This file allows you to specify a list of recommended extensions for your project. Users opening the project in VSCode will be prompted to install these recommended extensions.

launch.json: This file is used to configure debugging settings for your project. It defines how the VSCode debugger should launch and attach to your application for debugging purposes. It includes configurations for different scenarios such as running the application, running tests, etc.

tasks.json: This file is used to configure tasks that can be executed from within VSCode. For an Angular project, it might include tasks for building the application, running tests, or other custom tasks you want to define.

node_modules Directory: This directory contains the libraries and packages required by your project. It is generated and managed by npm (Node Package Manager).

src Directory: This is the main directory where your application's source code resides.

src/app Directory: This directory contains the components, modules, services, and other Angular-related files.

src/assets/ Directory: This directory is used to store static assets such as images, fonts, or other files that your application might need.

src/favicon.ico: Short for "favorite icon," is a small image or icon associated with the website. It is displayed in the browser's address bar, tabs, and bookmarks to help users easily identify and recognize a website.

src/index.html: The main HTML file that serves as the entry point for your Angular application.

7

```
∨ ELDARANGULAR
  ∨ .vscode
    {} extensions.json
    {} launch.json
    {} tasks.json
  > node_modules
  ∨ src
    ∨ app
      TS app-routing.module.ts
      <> app.component.html
      {} app.component.less
      TS app.component.ts
      TS app.module.server.ts
      TS app.module.ts
    ∨ assets
      ◈ .gitkeep
    ★ favicon.ico
    <> index.html
    TS main.server.ts
    TS main.ts
    {} styles.less
  ⚙ .editorconfig
  ◈ .gitignore
  {} angular.json
  {} package-lock.json
  {} package.json
  ⓘ README.md
  TS server.ts
  {} tsconfig.app.json
  TS tsconfig.json
  {} tsconfig.spec.json
```

src/main.server.ts: The entry point for the server-side rendering (SSR) of your Angular application.

src/main.ts: The main TypeScript file where the Angular application is bootstrapped. It imports the AppModule and calls platformBrowserDynamic().bootstrapModule(AppModule) to start the application.

src/styles.less: This file contains the global styles for your application. You can add your own styles or import external stylesheets here.

.editorconfig: Configuration file that defines and maintain consistent coding styles across different editors and IDEs for a particular project.

.gitignore: Specify untracked files that Git should ignore when working with a particular Git repository

angular.json: Configuration file for Angular CLI. It includes settings such as project name, output paths, and build configurations.

package.json and package-lock.json: These files manage project dependencies and scripts. package.json includes the list of dependencies, project metadata, and scripts for common tasks. package-lock.json contains the exact versions of dependencies to ensure consistent installations across different environments.

README.md: Markdown file that's provide essential information and documentation about the project to users, developers, or anyone else who interacts with the codebase. It's meant to be read first when someone explores the project.

server.ts: Angular Universal using Node.js and Express.js to serve the Angular application on the server (SSR)

tsconfig.json: TypeScript configuration file that specifies how TypeScript should compile the project.

tsconfig.app.json: Configure TypeScript compilation for the Angular application source code. It extends the main tsconfig.json file, inheriting its settings and allowing for additional configuration specific to the application.

tsconfig.spec.json: Configure TypeScript compilation for the unit tests, it extends the main tsconfig.json file, inheriting its settings and allowing for additional configuration specific to the tests.

Run the app

Use the ng serve command to start the development server. This will compile your Angular application and make it accessible at http://localhost:4200/ by default.

This command is part of the Angular CLI (Command Line Interface) and is used to start the development server for an Angular application.

```
ng serve
```

If you want the server to listen on a different port, you can specify it

```
ng serve --port 3000
```

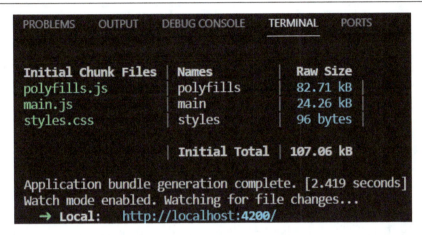

Hello, EldarAngular

Congratulations! Your app is running. 🎉

Explore the Docs ↗

Learn with Tutorials ↗

CLI Docs ↗

Angular Language Service ↗

Angular DevTools ↗

You can also use npm start command. The npm start command is a script defined in the scripts section of your package.json file. The actual behavior of npm start depends on how it's configured in your project.

```json
"scripts": {
    "ng": "ng",
    "start": "ng serve",
    "build": "ng build",
    "watch": "ng build --watch --configuration development",
    "test": "ng test",
    "serve:ssr:EldarAngular": "node dist/eldar-angular/server/server.mjs"
}
```

ng: This script defines a shorthand for the ng command, which is the Angular CLI. It allows you to use npm run ng instead of ng directly.

start: This script is used to start the development server using ng serve. The command npm start will execute ng serve.

build: This script is used to build the Angular application for production using ng build.

watch: This script is used to build the Angular application in watch mode, which means it will rebuild when changes are detected.

test: This script is used to run tests for the Angular application using ng test.

serve:ssr:EldarAngular: This script is specific to Angular Universal (Server-Side Rendering). It is used to start the server for server-side rendering. The command npm run serve:ssr:EldarAngular will execute node dist/eldar-angular/server/server.mjs.

In Angular, you typically do not need to rebuild the entire project every time you make a change in the code. The development server in Angular (ng serve) watches for changes in your source files after saving and automatically recompiles and refreshes the application in the browser.

App Folder

app-routing.module.ts: configure the routing for your Angular application. It defines the routes and their associated components, allowing navigation between different views.

app.component.html: The HTML template file for the root component (AppComponent). This file contains the structure and layout of the main component that represents the entire application.

app.component.less: LESS stylesheet associated with the root component. LESS is a CSS preprocessor that allows you to use variables, nesting, and other features to enhance your styling.

app.component.ts: The TypeScript file for the root component (AppComponent). It contains the logic and behavior associated with the root component, including any initialization, data binding, and other component-specific functionality.

app.module.server.ts: Server-side module configuration.

app.module.ts: The main Angular module file (AppModule). This file is crucial for bootstrapping your Angular application. It includes metadata about your application, such as the declarations (components, directives, pipes), imports (other modules), providers (services), and more.

Component

An Angular component is a reusable and self-contained piece of code that encapsulates a specific feature or functionality. Components are used to organize the user interface of an Angular application into modular and maintainable pieces.

Components are a type of directive with a template.

A component consists of three main files, class inside typescript file, html file and style file.

app.component.ts

```
import { Component } from '@angular/core';

@Component({
  selector: 'app-root',
  templateUrl: './app.component.html',
  styleUrl: './app.component.less'
})
export class AppComponent { }
```

<> app.component.html

{} app.component.less

TS app.component.ts

Template: The templateUrl property in the @Component decorator specifies the HTML content that represents the component's view. Templates can include Angular-specific syntax, such as data binding, directives, and event bindings.

Style: The styleUrl property in the @Component decorator specifies style file associated with the component. Styles can be defined using CSS or a preprocessor like SASS or LESS. When you want to include multiple style files for a component, you use the styleUrls property (with an "s") instead of styleUrl.

```
styleUrls: ['./app.component.less', './additional-styles.css']
```

app.component.html

```
<div class="hello">Hello</div>
```

app.component.less

```
.hello {
    color: red;
}
```

Selector: The selector property in the @Component decorator defines how the component will be identified in the HTML.

index.html

```
<body>
  <app-root></app-root>
</body>
```

The selector property is set to 'app-root', so Angular will look for occurrences of <app-root> in the HTML and replace them with the template and behavior defined in the AppComponent class. This is how Angular components are instantiated and integrated into the overall structure of the application.

While it's a common practice in Angular to use separate files for the template (HTML) and styles (CSS), it's not strictly required. You have the option to inline the template and styles directly within the @Component decorator.

Use the template and styles properties directly within the @Component decorator. This approach can be useful for small components or when the template and styles are closely related to the component logic.

app.component.ts

```
@Component({
  selector: 'app-root',
  template: `<div class="hello">Hello</div>`,
  styles: `.hello {
    color: red;
}`
})

export class AppComponent {
}
```

To make an Angular component usable in your application, you need to declare it in an Angular module. In Angular, modules are used to organize and configure the application. Each module can declare a set of components, directives, pipes, and other related artifacts.

app.module.ts

```typescript
@NgModule({
  declarations: [
    AppComponent
  ],
  imports: [
    BrowserModule,
    AppRoutingModule
  ],
  providers: [
    provideClientHydration()
  ],
  bootstrap: [AppComponent]
})
export class AppModule { }
```

declarations: This is where you list all the components, directives, and pipes that belong to this module. Make sure to include your AppComponent in the declarations array.

imports: This is where you import other Angular modules that this module depends on. In this case, the BrowserModule and AppRoutingModule is imported.

bootstrap: This property specifies the root component that Angular should bootstrap when the application starts. In this case, AppComponent is set as the root component.

Create a component

You can create a component manually by creating the files or using Angular CLI:

```
ng generate component my-component
```

This command will create a new folder named "my-component" with the necessary files and configurations for your Angular component.

```
PS C:\1\apps\EldarAngular\src\app\components> ng generate component my-component
CREATE src/app/components/my-component/my-component.component.html (28 bytes)
CREATE src/app/components/my-component/my-component.component.spec.ts (660 bytes)
CREATE src/app/components/my-component/my-component.component.ts (233 bytes)
CREATE src/app/components/my-component/my-component.component.less (0 bytes)
UPDATE src/app/app.module.ts (564 bytes)
```

Angular CLI has added an HTML file, a TypeScript (ts) file, a Less file, and a spec.ts file for the MyComponent. The .spec.ts file is conventionally used for writing unit tests for components. Additionally, Angular CLI automatically added MyComponent to the declarations section in the app.module.ts file.

Let's use my-component inside app component:

app.component.html

```html
<my-component></my-component>
```

Standalone Component

A standalone component is a component that is developed and utilized independently, without being part of a larger Angular application. Standalone components eliminate the need for NgModules, reducing boilerplate code and making development more streamlined.

```typescript
@Component({
   selector: 'my-component',
   templateUrl: './my-component.component.html',
   styleUrl: './my-component.component.less',
   standalone: true,
})
export class MyComponent { }
```

Mark the component with the standalone flag, this flag tells the Angular compiler that the component doesn't need an NgModule.

When using a standalone component, you add the component to the 'imports' section of app.module.ts instead of the 'declarations' section.

When you need to use logic from different code into a standalone component, use the 'imports' field inside the component.

```typescript
Component({
   selector: 'my-component',
   standalone: true,
   imports:[SomeModule, SomeComponent]
})
```

View Encapsulation

View encapsulation is the way Angular isolates styles for a component. It is a feature that allows you to define how styles defined in a component affect the rest of the application. Angular provides 3 view encapsulation strategies:

Emulated (Default): Scoped to that component only. Styles will be available only to this component.

None: Styles are not encapsulated. Styles will affect the entire application and may lead to global styles.

ShadowDom: Angular uses the browser's Shadow DOM to encapsulate styles. The styles are applied to the Shadow DOM of the component, ensuring isolation.

Emulated and ShadowDom achieve a similar outcome, they both isolate the styles of a component from the rest of the application. However, they differ in the underlying techniques they use to achieve this isolation, and these differences may have implications depending on the specific requirements and browser support of your project.

To specify the encapsulation strategy for a component, you use the encapsulation property in the @Component decorator:

```typescript
import { Component, ViewEncapsulation } from '@angular/core';

@Component({
  selector: 'my-component',
  templateUrl: './my-component.component.html',
  styleUrl: './my-component.component.less',
  encapsulation: ViewEncapsulation.None
 //encapsulation: ViewEncapsulation.Emulated
 //encapsulation: ViewEncapsulation.ShadowDom
})
export class MyComponent { }
```

Global Styles

Global styles are applied throughout the entire application, impacting all components and disregarding ViewEncapsulation.

::ng-deep

The ::ng-deep selector is a special Angular combinator that pierces through the encapsulation provided by the ViewEncapsulation mechanism. It allows you to apply styles to the components and elements within a component, even if they are encapsulated with Emulated or Shadow DOM encapsulation.

```
::ng-deep .custom-class { color: red;}
```

In this example, the ::ng-deep selector is used to apply styles to elements with the class .custom-class within the component, even if they are encapsulated.

Global Styles File

Open your angular.json file.

Locate the "styles" array within the "build" options of your project configuration.

Add the path to your global styles file to the "styles" array.

Create a global styles file, for example, styles.less, in the specified location (e.g., src folder).

```
.custom-class { color: red;}
```

Now, the styles defined in styles.less will be applied globally across your application.

Template

A template is a blueprint for a segment of a user interface. It extending the HTML syntax with additional functionality. Templates are written in HTML enhanced with Angular syntax. This extension of HTML includes features such as data binding, event handling, and Angular-specific directives, enabling the creation of dynamic and interactive applications.

Binding

In Angular, a binding establishes a dynamic connection between a UI created from a template and the associated model (component instance). This live connection facilitates synchronization between the view and the model, allowing seamless updates in both directions. Bindings are used to reflect changes in the model in the view and vice versa, responding to user actions or events. Angular's Change Detection algorithm ensures continuous synchronization between the view and model, maintaining a responsive and up-to-date user interface.

Interpolation

Interpolation is a way to bind data from the component to the view (HTML) in an Angular application. It is achieved using double curly braces {{ }} in the template. This syntax is also known as "mustache syntax."

app.component.ts

```
@Component({
  selector: 'app-root',
  templateUrl: './app.component.html',
  styleUrl: './app.component.less',
})

export class AppComponent {
  message = 'Hello Eldar';
  imageUrl = 'my-image.jpg';
}
```

app.component.html

```
<div>{{message}}</div>
<img src="{{imageUrl}}" >
```

Result

{{ message }} is an interpolation expression. It gets replaced by the value of the message property from the component, resulting in the following rendered HTML:

```
<div>Hello Eldar</div>
<img src="my-image.jpg">
```

Property binding

Property binding is a mechanism in Angular that allows you to bind a property of a DOM element, directive, or component to a property in the component class. It enables you to dynamically set or update the value of a property in the view based on a corresponding property in the component.

The syntax for property binding uses square brackets [] within the template.

```
export class AppComponent {
  imageUrl = 'my-image.jpg';
}
```

```
<img [src]="imageUrl" >
```

In this example, the src property of the img element is bound to the imageUrl property in the component class.

Attribute binding

When property binding syntax ([property]="value") is not applicable, or if you need to bind to an attribute that doesn't have a corresponding property, you can use attribute binding with the

Attribute binding allows you to dynamically set the value of an HTML attribute based on a property or expression in your Angular component. This is achieved using the square bracket syntax [attr.attributeName]="value".

```
<div [attr.data-custom]="myValue"></div>
```

In this example data-custom is an attribute, [attr.data-custom] allows you to dynamically set the value of the data-custom attribute based on the value of the myValue property in your component.

```
<select [attr.multiple]="true ? '' : null">
```

In the provided example, If the condition is true, the multiple attribute will be added; otherwise, it will be omitted.

Class and style binding

Class and style binding allows you to dynamically set CSS classes and styles based on conditions or properties in your component. These bindings provide a way to manage the appearance and behavior of HTML elements in a dynamic and data-driven manner.

Binding a CSS class conditionally based on a property in the component.

```
<div [class.my-class]="isMyClass"></div>
```

Multiple Classes:

```
<div [class.my-class]="isMyClass" [class.my-class2]="isMyClass2" ></div>
```

Binding the color style property dynamically:

```
<div [style.color]="dynamicColor"></div>
```

Multiple Styles:

```
<div [style.color]="dynamicColor" [style.fontSize.px]="fontSize" ></div>
```

Event binding

Event binding allows you to capture and respond to user actions or events in your application. It enables you to handle events such as button clicks, mouse movements, key presses, and more, triggering corresponding methods or expressions in your component.

```
<button (click)="hello()">click</button>
```

```
export class AppComponent {
  hello() {
    alert("hello");
  }
}
```

In this example, "hello()" is a template statement. It listens for the click event on the button and, when triggered, calls the hello method from the component.

Event binding can be used with various events such as: (dblclick), (mouseover), (mouseout), (mousedown), (mouseup), (keydown), (keyup), (keypress), (change), (submit), (focus), (blur), (touchstart), (touchstart), (touchend), (touchend), (dragstart), (dragover), (drop).

$event object

The $event object is a special variable that represents the event object associated with a particular DOM event. It allows you to access information about the event, such as the event type, target element, and other relevant details. The $event variable is commonly used in event bindings to pass event data to the handler method in the component.

```
<input type="button" (click)="func($event)" value="hi">
```

```
export class AppComponent {
  func(event: any) {
    let val = event.target.value; // hi
  }
}
```

```
PointerEvent
  tangentialPressure: 0
▶ target: button
  tiltX: 0
  tiltY: 0
  timeStamp: 60744.5999
  toElement: null
  twist: 0
  type: "click"
▶ view: Window {window:
  which: 1
  width: 1
  x: 33
  y: 25
```

Two-way binding [(ngModel)]

Two-way binding in Angular provides a convenient way to synchronize the data between a component's property and an input field or other UI element. It allows changes to the property to automatically update the UI, and conversely, changes in the UI to update the property.

[(ngModel)] is the syntax for two-way binding.

For two-way binding to work, you need to do the following:

Import the FormsModule from @angular/forms in your Angular module.

Include the FormsModule in the imports array of your @NgModule decorator.

```
import { FormsModule } from '@angular/forms';

export class AppComponent {
  text: string = '';
}
```

```
<input [(ngModel)]="text" />
{{ text }}
```

In this example, any changes made in the input field will be automatically reflected in the text property, and vice versa. Two-way binding simplifies the process of keeping the UI and the component's state in sync.

Eldar   Eldar

Template statements

Template statements are expressions or code snippets written in the template that respond to events or user interactions. They are used for handling actions like button clicks, mouse events, key presses, and other user-triggered events. Angular uses a set of event binding syntax to capture these events in the template and execute corresponding methods or expressions in the component. The syntax for a template statement generally involves enclosing the event within parentheses, followed by the assignment of the component's method or expression.

Template statements use language similar to JavaScript, but they have their own parser and some specific rules.

```
<button (click)="count = count + 1">click</button>
```

In this example, the (click) event is bound to a template statement that increments the count variable.

```
<div [style.color]="isActive ? 'green' : 'red'">Dynamic Color</div>
```

This is a ternary operator that evaluates the value of isActive. If isActive is true, the color is set to 'green'; otherwise, it's set to 'red'.

Differences in Parsers: Template statements in Angular have a separate parser from template expressions. While both use a syntax resembling JavaScript, they are parsed differently.

Supported Operations: Template statements support basic assignment (=) and chaining expressions with semicolons (;).

Not Allowed JavaScript inside Template Expression: Certain JavaScript features and syntax are not allowed in template statements include:

The use of the new keyword.

Increment and decrement operators, such as ++ and --.

Operator assignment, like += and -=.

Bitwise operators, such as | and &.

The pipe operator (|) is not allowed in template statements.

Template variables

Template variables allow you to capture a reference to an element, you define a template variable using the hash (#) symbol.

```
export class AppComponent {
  send(email: string) {

  }
}
```

```
<input #emailInput type="text">
<button (click)="send(emailInput.value)">Send</button>
```

In this example, #emailInput is a template variable that refers to the input element. When the button is clicked, the send function is called with the value of the input field.

Pipe |

A pipe allows you to transform and format data in your templates. Pipes are used to apply various transformations to the data before displaying it in the view. Angular provides a set of built-in pipes, and you can also create custom pipes.

For full pipes documentary: https://angular.io/guide/pipes-overview

{{ expression | pipeName : arg1 : arg2 : ... }}:

The expression is the data you want to transform.

pipeName is the name of the pipe you want to apply.

arg1, arg2, etc., are optional arguments that you can pass to the pipe.

Date Pipe

Formats a date value according to locale rules.

```
import { Pipe, PipeTransform } from '@angular/core';

export class AppComponent {
  currentDate = new Date();
}
```

```
<div>{{ currentDate }}</div>
```
Wed Jan 31 2024 20:17:51 GMT+0200 (שעון ישראל (חורף))

```
<div>{{ currentDate | date:'dd.MM.yyyy HH:mm:ss' }}</div>
```
31.01.2024 20:15:41

```
<div>{{ currentDate | date:'HH:mm:ss.ssss zzzz' }}</div>
```
20:15:41.4141 GMT+02:00

```
<div>{{ currentDate | date:'short' }}</div>
```
1/31/24, 8:15 PM

```
<div>{{ currentDate | date:'medium' }}</div>
```
Jan 31, 2024, 8:15:41 PM

```
<div>{{ currentDate | date:'long' }}</div>
```
January 31, 2024 at 8:15:41 PM GMT+2

```
<div>{{ currentDate | date:'full' }}</div>
```
Wednesday, January 31, 2024 at 8:15:41 PM GMT+02:00

```
<div>{{ currentDate | date:'shortDate' }}</div>
```
1/31/24

```
<div>{{ currentDate | date:'mediumDate' }}</div>
```
Jan 31, 2024

```
<div>{{ currentDate | date:'longDate' }}</div>
```
January 31, 2024

```
<div>{{ currentDate | date:'fullDate' }}</div>
```
Wednesday, January 31, 2024

```
<div>{{ currentDate | date:'shortTime' }}</div>
```
8:15 PM

```
<div>{{ currentDate | date:'mediumTime' }}</div>
```
8:15:41 PM

```
<div>{{ currentDate | date:'longTime' }}</div>
```
8:15:41 PM GMT+2

```
<div>{{ currentDate | date:'fullTime' }}</div>
```
8:15:41 PM GMT+02:00

Upper Case Pipe

Transforms text to all uppercase.

```
{{ 'Eldar' | uppercase }}
```
ELDAR

Lower Case Pipe

Transforms text to all lowercase.

```
{{ 'Eldar' | lowercase }}
```
eldar

Currency Pipe

Transforms a number to a currency string, formatted according to locale rules.

Currency code according ISO 4217.

```
{{ 1.2 | currency:'USD' }}
```
$1.20
```
{{ 1.2 | currency:'ILS' }}
```
₪1.20
```
{{ 1.2 | currency:'AUD' }}
```
A$1.20
```
{{ 1.2 | currency:'CAD' }}
```
CA$1.20
```
{{ 1.2 | currency:'GBP' }}
```
£1.20

Decimal Pipe

Transforms a number into a string with a decimal point, formatted according to locale rules.

{MinIntegerDigits}.{MinFractionDigits}-{MaxFractionDigits}

MinIntegerDigits: The minimum number of integer digits before the decimal point. Default is 1.

MinFractionDigits: The minimum number of digits after the decimal point. Default is 0.

MaxFractionDigits: The maximum number of digits after the decimal point. Default is 3.

```
{{123.456 | number: '1.0-0'}}
```
123
```
{{123.456 | number: '1.0-1'}}
```
123.5
```
{{123.456 | number: '1.0-2'}}
```
123.46
```
{{123.456 | number: '1.0-3'}}
```
123.456

Percent Pipe

Transforms a number to a percentage string, formatted according to locale rules.

Decimal representation options, specified by a string in the following format:

{MinIntegerDigits}.{MinFractionDigits}-{MaxFractionDigits}.

MinIntegerDigits: The minimum number of integer digits before the decimal point. Default is 1.

MinFractionDigits: The minimum number of digits after the decimal point. Default is 0.

MaxFractionDigits: The maximum number of digits after the decimal point. Default is 0.

```
{{ 0 | percent }}
```
0%
```
{{ 2 | percent }}
```
200%
```
{{ 2.5 | percent }}
```
250%
```
{{ 0.5 | percent }}
```
50%
```
{{ 0.05 | percent }}
```
5%
```
{{ 5 | percent:'1.0-0' }}
```
500%
```
{{ 5 | percent:'5.3-3' }}
```
00,500.000%

Async Pipe

Subscribe and unsubscribe to an asynchronous source such as an observable.

```
import { Observable, of } from 'rxjs';

export class AppComponent {
  data: Observable<string> = of('Hello Eldar AsyncPipe');
}
```

```
{{ data | async }}
```
Hello Eldar AsyncPipe

The async pipe automatically subscribes to the data Observable and updates the view whenever new data is emitted. It also takes care of unsubscribing when the component is destroyed, preventing memory leaks.

Json Pipe

Display a component object property to the screen as JSON for debugging.

```
export class AppComponent {
  obj = { firstName: 'Eldar', lastName: 'Cohen' }
}
```

```
{{ obj | json }}
```
{ "firstName": "Eldar", "lastName": "Cohen" }

Chained pipes

You can chain multiple pipes together to create a sequence of transformations.

```
{{ 'Eldar' | uppercase | lowercase }}
```
Eldar

Pipe precedence

When you use multiple pipes, the order of the pipes matters. Angular processes the pipes from left to right, and the result of each pipe becomes the input for the next one. This sequence is important because the output of one pipe serves as the input to the next.

When using the ternary operator (?:) and pipes, it's crucial to be aware of the operator precedence to avoid unexpected results. The pipe operator (|) has higher precedence than the ternary operator. This means that when combining the ternary operator and pipes, you may need to use parentheses to ensure the correct order of evaluation. Without parentheses, the pipe might be applied to the result of the ternary operation in an unexpected way.

Create custom pipe

To create a custom pipe, you need to implement the PipeTransform interface.

Let's create a custom pipe that transforms the input value to uppercase.

```typescript
@Pipe({
  name: 'toUpperCase'
})
export class ToUpperCasePipe implements PipeTransform {
  transform(value: any, arg1?: any, arg2?: any): any {
    return value.toUpperCase();
  }
}
```

```typescript
@NgModule({
  declarations: [
    AppComponent,
    ToUpperCasePipe
  ]

      .

      .

      .

})
```

```
{{ 'Eldar' | toUpperCase }}
```
ELDAR

Sharing data between components

In Angular, there are several ways to share data between components.

@Input()

The @Input() is a decorator that allows you to pass data from a parent component to a child component. By using @Input(), you expose a property in the child component that can receive values from the parent component.

child.component.ts

```typescript
import { Component, Input} from '@angular/core';
@Component({
  selector: 'child',
  templateUrl: './child.component.html'
})
export class ChildComponent {

  @Input() data: any;
}
```

parent.component.html

```html
<child [data]="123"></child>
```

In this example, the @Input() decorator is used to create an input property named data in the ChildComponent. This property will be bound to a property in the parent component.

@Ouput()

The @Output() is a decorator that allows you to pass data from a child component to a parent component. By using @Output() property in the child component you can emit events that a parent component can listen to and respond to.

child.component.ts

```typescript
import { Component, EventEmitter, Output } from '@angular/core';

@Component({
  selector: 'child',
  templateUrl: './child.component.html'
})
export class ChildComponent {
  @Output() dataToParent = new EventEmitter<any>();

  send() {
    this.dataToParent.emit('Data from Child');
  }
}
```

child.component.html

```html
<button (click)="send()">Send</button>
```

parent.component.ts

```typescript
export class ParentComponent {

  receiveDataFromChild(data: any) {
    console.log(data);
  }
}
```

parent.component.html

```html
<child (dataToParent)="receiveDataFromChild($event)"></child>
```

In this example, the ChildComponent has an @Output() property named dataToParent, which is an instance of EventEmitter. The send() method emits an event with a string message.

In the parent component's template, (dataToParent)="receiveDataFromChild($event)" listens for the event emitted by the child component. The receiveDataFromChild() method is called whenever the child component emits the event.

This way, the child component can communicate with its parent by emitting events, and the parent can respond to those events.

@ViewChild

The @ViewChild decorator is used to gain access to a child component, directive, or element in the template. It allows a parent component to interact with its child components by accessing their properties or calling their methods or elements by obtaining a reference to them.

parent.component.ts

```typescript
import { AfterViewInit, Component, ViewChild } from '@angular/core';
import { ChildComponent } from './components/my-component/child.component';

export class ParentComponent {

  @ViewChild(ChildComponent)
  private childComponent!: ChildComponent;

  ngAfterViewInit() {
    this.childComponent!.myVar = "Hi";
    this.childComponent!.print();
  }
}
```

parent.component.html

```html
<child></child>
```

child.component.ts

```typescript
export class ChildComponent {

  myVar: string = '';
  print() { console.log('Hello'); }
}
```

In ngAfterViewInit, you set the myVar property of the ChildComponent to "Hi" and call the print() method. This demonstrates how the parent component can interact with its child components after they have been initialized.

Service

A service is a singleton object that can be used to encapsulate and share functionality across components, directives, and other services. Services play a crucial role in organizing and managing the application's business logic, data, and other shared functionalities.

To create service, you can create ts file or use cli command:

`ng generate service serviceName`

```
import { Injectable } from '@angular/core';

@Injectable({
    providedIn: 'root'
})
export class AppService {
    private data: any;


    getSharedData() {
        return this.data;
    }

    setSharedData(data: any): void {
        this.data = data;
    }
}
```

In this example, AppService is created with the @Injectable decorator, and it's provided at the root level (providedIn: 'root'). This makes it a singleton service available throughout the application.

The providedIn property in the @Injectable decorator is used to configure the Angular dependency injection system to provide a service instance at a specific level of the application. The values for providedIn are:

'root': The service is provided at the application level, creating a singleton instance shared across the entire application. This is the most common option for services that should have a single, shared instance throughout the app.

'platform': The service is provided at the platform level, creating a singleton instance shared by all Angular applications on the page. This is less common and is typically used in advanced scenarios where services need to be shared across multiple applications on the same page.

The default value for providedIn is null, which means that the service must be provided explicitly in the providers array of an Angular module.

Using the service in a component:

```
import { AppService } from './app.service';

export class AppComponent {

  constructor(private appService: AppService) {

    appService.setSharedData(1);
    console.log(appService.getSharedData());


  }
}
```

In this example, AppComponent injects AppService in its constructor and uses it to access and modify the shared data. The setSharedData() method updates the data variable in the service and reflects the changes in the component's template.

Dependency Injection

Dependency Injection is a design pattern in which a class receives its dependencies from an external source rather than creating them itself. In the context of Angular, it is a mechanism by which Angular's injector provides instances of services to components or other services.

Injecting AppService in AppComponent constructor:

```typescript
export class AppComponent {

  constructor(private appService: AppService) {

  }
}
```

In the AppComponent constructor, the AppService is injected as a parameter. This means that an instance of AppService will be provided to the AppComponent by Angular's dependency injection system when an instance of AppComponent is created.

Directives

Directives allows you to extend and manipulate the Document Object Model (DOM) in your application. Directives are markers on a DOM element that tell Angular to attach a specific behavior to that element or its children. There are three main types of directives in Angular: Component Directives, Attribute Directives, and Structural Directives.

Attribute Directives

Attribute directives are used to change the appearance or behavior of a DOM element by adding or removing attributes. Angular provides some built-in attribute directives.

NgModel is an attribute directive.

[ngClass]

The ngClass allows you to dynamically set CSS classes on an HTML element based on the evaluation of certain expressions.

```
<div [ngClass]="true ? 'red' : ''">Eldar</div>
```

Since the condition is true, the 'red' class will be applied to the <div> element. If the condition were false, no additional class would be applied.

Result:

```
<div class="red">Eldar</div>
```

Using an object literal to define multiple classes based on conditions

```
<div [ngClass]="{'red': true, 'my-font': true}">Eldar</div>
```

The <div> element will have both the 'red' and 'my-font' classes applied. If any of the conditions were false, the corresponding class would not be applied.

Result:

```
<div class="red my-font">Eldar</div>
```

Usage of ngClass in combination with a method to return the class object

```
export class AppComponent {
  getClasses() {
    return { 'red': true, 'my-font': true };
  }
}
```

```
<div [ngClass]="getClasses()">Eldar</div>
```

[ngStyle]

The ngStyle directive is used to dynamically set inline styles for HTML elements. Similar to ngClass, ngStyle allows you to apply styles based on certain conditions or dynamic values.

```
export class AppComponent {
  getStyles() {
    return {
      'background-color': 'yellow',
      'font-style': 'italic'
    };
  }
}
```

```
<div [ngStyle]="getStyles()">Eldar</div>        Eldar
```

```
<div [ngStyle]="{'background-color': 1==1 ? 'red' : 'yellow' }">Eldar</div>
                                                      Eldar
```

Structural Directives

Structural directives modify the structure of the DOM by adding, removing, or manipulating elements. They are prefixed with an asterisk (*) in the HTML.

*ngIf

The *ngIf directive is a structural directive that conditionally adds or removes elements from the DOM based on a specified expression. It's commonly used to control the visibility of elements in your Angular templates. You can use various types of conditions in the *ngIf directive, such as boolean variables, expressions, or methods that return a boolean value.

```
export class AppComponent {
  isVisible = true;
  isShow() {
    return true;
  }
}
```

```
<div *ngIf="true">1</div>          1
<div *ngIf="false">2</div>         3
<div *ngIf="isVisible">3</div>     4
<div *ngIf="isShow()">4</div>
```

The first div with *ngIf="true" will always be displayed because the condition is true.

The second div with *ngIf="false" will never be displayed because the condition is false.

The third div with *ngIf="isVisible" will be displayed because the isVisible variable is true.

The fourth div with *ngIf="isShow()" will be displayed because the isShow() method returns true.

*ngFor

The *ngFor directive is a structural directive used for iterating over a collection of data and rendering HTML elements for each item in the collection. It is commonly used with arrays or other iterable objects to create dynamic lists of elements.

```
<div *ngFor="let item of [1,2,3]">{{item}}</div>
```

*ngFor directive is used to loop through each element in the array [1, 2, 3]. For each iteration, it creates a <div> element, and the content of the <div> is the value of the current item. The result, when rendered, will be three <div> elements with the values 1, 2, and 3, respectively.

```
<div>1</div>
<div>2</div>
<div>3</div>
```
1
2
3

index

You can get the index of the current iteration when using *ngFor by using the built-in index variable. The index is zero-based.

```
<div *ngFor="let item of [1,2,3]; let i=index">
    {{i}}-{{item}}
</div>
```
0-1
1-2
2-3

trackBy

Using trackBy is beneficial when dealing with dynamic lists where items can be added, removed, or rearranged. It helps Angular avoid unnecessary re-rendering of DOM elements, resulting in better performance.

```
export class AppComponent {

  items = [1, 2, 3];

  trackByItems(index: number, item: any): any {
    return item.id; // unique identifier for tracking changes
  }

}
```

```
<div *ngFor="let item of items; trackBy: trackByItems">{{ item }}</div>
```

Without trackBy, Angular has to assume that the identity of each item is based on the array index. When the array changes (e.g., an item is added or removed), Angular assumes all elements have potentially changed, leading to complete DOM element replacement.

When you provide a trackBy function, Angular uses the return value of this function to track the identity of each item. If the identity doesn't change (as long as the trackBy function returns the same value for an item before and after changes), Angular can update only the parts of the DOM that are affected by the changes, rather than replacing the entire elements.

*ngSwitch

The *ngSwitch directive is used for conditionally displaying content based on the value of an expression. It's a convenient way to handle multiple cases within a template.

```
export class AppComponent {
  item = 1;
}
```

```
<div [ngSwitch]="item">
    <div *ngSwitchCase="1">Content for case 1</div>
    <div *ngSwitchCase="2">Content for case 2</div>
    <div *ngSwitchCase="3">Content for case 3</div>
    <div *ngSwitchDefault>Default content</div>
</div>
```

Result: Content for case 1

[ngSwitch]: Binds the expression to the ngSwitch directive.

*ngSwitchCase: Defines a case for a specific value.

*ngSwitchDefault: Defines the default case.

Multiple template bindings on one element

Structural directives have a limit to only one structural directive per HTML element.

```
<div *ngIf="1" *ngFor="let item of [1,2,3]"></div>
```

Error message: Can't have multiple template bindings on one element. Use only one attribute prefixed with *.

To resolve this issue, you should separate the structural directives onto different HTML elements. For example:

```
<div *ngIf="1">
  <div *ngFor="let item of [1,2,3]"></div>
</div>
```

<ng-container>

You can use <ng-container> when you need to apply multiple structural directives without introducing additional elements into the DOM. <ng-container> is a special Angular element that doesn't create a new element in the DOM, making it useful for structural directives that require a single parent element.

```
<ng-container *ngIf="1">
    <div *ngFor="let item of [1,2,3]"></div>
</ng-container>
```

Create Attribute Directive

You can use angular cli command or manually create the file.

`ng generate directive myDirective`

This directive allows you to dynamically set the background color of an element by applying the [backgroundColor] attribute to it. The color can be provided through the backgroundColor input property, and the directive reacts to changes in this property using the ngOnChanges lifecycle hook.

```typescript
import { Directive, ElementRef, Input, OnChanges, SimpleChanges }
from '@angular/core';

@Directive({
  standalone: true,
  selector: '[backgroundColor]',
})
export class BackgroundColorDirective implements OnChanges {
  @Input() backgroundColor: string = '';

  constructor(private el: ElementRef) {
    this.setBackgroundColor(this.backgroundColor);
  }

  ngOnChanges(changes: SimpleChanges): void {
    if (changes['backgroundColor']) {
      this.setBackgroundColor(changes['backgroundColor'].currentValue);
    }
  }

  private setBackgroundColor(color: string) {
    this.el.nativeElement.style.backgroundColor = color;
  }
}
```

```html
<div [backgroundColor]="'red'">Eldar</div>
```
Eldar

@Directive: Decorator used to annotate the class as an Angular directive.

standalone: true: Indicates that this directive is standalone (not associated with a component).

selector: '[backgroundColor]': Defines the attribute selector for this directive. The directive can be applied to elements with the attribute backgroundColor.

ngOnChanges: Lifecycle hook method called when input properties change.

changes: SimpleChanges: Object containing the changed input properties.

if (changes.backgroundColor): Checks if the backgroundColor input property has changed.

this.setBackgroundColor(changes.backgroundColor.currentValue): Updates the background color based on the new value of the backgroundColor input property.

this.el.nativeElement.style.backgroundColor = color: Accesses the native element and sets its background color.

Create Structural Directive

In this example, the *appRepeat structural directive is used to repeat the content inside the div three times.

```typescript
import { Directive, Input, TemplateRef, ViewContainerRef } from
'@angular/core';

@Directive({
  selector: '[appRepeat]'
})
export class RepeatDirective {
  constructor(
    private templateRef: TemplateRef<any>,
    private viewContainer: ViewContainerRef
  ) { }

  @Input() set appRepeat(times: number) {
    this.viewContainer.clear();

    for (let i = 0; i < times; i++) {
      this.viewContainer.createEmbeddedView(this.templateRef);
    }
  }
}
```

```html
<div *appRepeat="3">This will be repeated three times</div>
```

@Input() set appRepeat(times: number): This is a setter method for the appRepeat property. It's annotated with @Input(), making it an input property that can be bound in the template. The method is triggered whenever the appRepeat property is updated.

TemplateRef: Represents the template contents.

ViewContainerRef: Represents a container where one or more views can be attached.

this.viewContainer.clear(): Clears any existing views from the view container.

this.viewContainer.createEmbeddedView(this.templateRef): Creates an embedded view based on the template reference (this.templateRef) and adds it to the view container.

51

Directive composition

Directive composition simplifies the reuse of common behaviors across components and directives. Achieves this by allowing you to apply directives directly to a component's host element. Enhances code organization, maintainability, and testability.

@HostBinding

The @HostBinding is a decorator that allows you to bind a directive property to a host element property. This means you can set properties of the element that hosts your directive from within the directive class.

directive.ts

```typescript
import { Directive, HostBinding } from '@angular/core';

@Directive({
  selector: '[backgroundColor]'
})
export class BackgroundColorDirective {

  @HostBinding('style.backgroundColor') color: string = 'red';
}
```

another component that wants to use

```html
<div backgroundColor>hello</div>
```
hello

In this example, we've added the backgroundColor directive to the <div> element in the template. Now, when you run your Angular application and navigate to the component that uses this directive, the background color of the <div> element will be set to red due to the BackgroundColorDirective.

@HostListener

The @HostListener is a decorator that allows you to listen for events on the host element of a directive.

directive.ts

```typescript
import { Directive, ElementRef, HostListener } from '@angular/core';

@Directive({
  selector: '[backgroundColor]'
})
export class BackgroundColorDirective {

  constructor(private el: ElementRef) { }

  @HostListener('click') onClick() {
    this.el.nativeElement.style.backgroundColor = 'red'
  }
}
```

another component that wants to use

```html
<div backgroundColor>hello</div>
```
hello

When you click on the <div>, the onClick method in the BackgroundColorDirective will be triggered, and it will set the background color of the <div> to red. The directive provides a way to encapsulate and reuse this behavior across different components, promoting modularity and maintainability in your Angular application.

Dynamic component loading

Dynamic component loading allows you to load components dynamically at runtime. This is useful when you want to create flexible and dynamic user interfaces or load components based on certain conditions.

parent.component.ts

```typescript
import { Component, ViewContainerRef } from '@angular/core';
import { ChildComponent } from './components/my-component/child.component';

export class ParentComponent {

  constructor(private viewContainerRef: ViewContainerRef) {
    viewContainerRef.createComponent(ChildComponent);
  }

}
```

child.component.html

```html
Hello
```

When an instance of ParentComponent is created, it uses the ViewContainerRef to dynamically create an instance of ChildComponent and insert it into the view. As a result, the content of ChildComponent (in this case, the "Hello" text) will be displayed in the view where the AppComponent is rendered.

To close the ChildComponent after creating it within the ParentComponent, you need to capture a reference to the dynamically created component and then call its destroy() method.

```typescript
import { Component, ViewContainerRef, ComponentRef } from '@angular/core';
import { ChildComponent } from './components/my-component/child.component';

export class ParentComponent {

  childComponentRef: ComponentRef<ChildComponent>;

  constructor(private viewContainerRef: ViewContainerRef) {

    this.childComponentRef = viewContainerRef.createComponent(ChildComponent);

  }

  closeChildComponent() {
    // Check if the child component reference exists
    if (this.childComponentRef) {
      // Destroy the child component
      this.childComponentRef.destroy();
    }
  }

}
```

Render HTML

```
export class UserComponent {
  html = '<div>Hello</div>';
}
```

```
{{html}}
```

Browser UI Result

Hello

Angular does not render HTML content by default when using this syntax for security reasons, to prevent Cross-Site Scripting (XSS) attacks.

If you want to render HTML content, you should use the [innerHTML] property binding.

[innerHTML]

```
<div [innerHTML]="html"></div>
```

Browser UI Result

Hello

DomSanitizer

Angular blocks the binding of dynamic HTML content by default for security reasons, even when using the [innerHTML] property. This behavior is designed to prevent Cross-Site Scripting (XSS) attacks.

The DomSanitizer service helps prevent security issues when working with dynamic content. You can use it to sanitize and bind HTML content.

```
import { DomSanitizer, SafeHtml } from "@angular/platform-browser";

export class MyComponent {

  sanitizedHtml: SafeHtml;

  constructor(private sanitizer: DomSanitizer) {
   let dynamicHtml = this.getHtmlFromServer();
   this.sanitizedHtml = this.sanitizer.bypassSecurityTrustHtml(dynamicHtml);
  }

  getHtmlFromServer() { return '<div>Hello</div>'; }
}
```

```
<div [innerHTML]="sanitizedHtml"></div>
```

The getHtmlFromServer method simulates fetching HTML content from the server.

Inside the constructor, the getHtmlFromServer method is called to retrieve dynamic HTML content, and bypassSecurityTrustHtml method of DomSanitizer is used to mark the HTML content as safe. The key here is the use of DomSanitizer.bypassSecurityTrustHtml to explicitly declare that the HTML content is trusted. This helps mitigate the risk of XSS attacks by indicating to Angular that you have ensured the content is safe to be rendered as HTML.

Renderer2/ElementRef

Renderer2 is a service that provides a way to interact with the DOM (Document Object Model) directly. It's part of the Renderer abstraction, which Angular uses to render views. Renderer2 can be used to create and append elements dynamically.

ElementRef represents a reference to a DOM element within a component. It is used to access and interact with the underlying native element that an Angular component represents.

```typescript
import {ElementRef, Renderer2 } from "@angular/core";

export class UserComponent {

  constructor(private renderer: Renderer2, private el: ElementRef) {
    // Creates an element
    const div = renderer.createElement('div');

    // Appends a child element to a parent element
    renderer.appendChild(this.el.nativeElement, div);

    // Sets an attribute on an element
    renderer.setAttribute(div, 'class', 'example-class');

    // Adds a CSS class to an element
    renderer.addClass(div, 'example-class');

    // Removes a CSS class from an element
    renderer.removeClass(div, 'example-class');

    // Listens for events on an element.
    renderer.listen(div, 'click', (event) => {
      console.log('Element clicked', event);
    });
  }

}
```

Routes

Routes are used to navigate between different components and views in a single-page application (SPA). The Angular Router is a powerful tool for managing navigation in your application.

Add AppRoutingModule to AppModule:

app.module.ts

```
import { AppRoutingModule } from './app-routing.module';
import { AppComponent} from './app.component';
import { UserComponent } from './components/user/user.component';
import { HomeComponent } from './components/home/home.component';

@NgModule({
  declarations: [
    AppComponent,
    UserComponent,
    HomeComponent
  ],
  imports: [
    AppRoutingModule
  ]
})
export class AppModule { }
```

<router-outlet>

Add <router-outlet> directive to AppComponent:

app.component.html

```
<router-outlet></router-outlet>
```

The <router-outlet> is a directive that serves as a placeholder where the router renders the component views based on the current route. It acts as a container where the content of the routed components is dynamically loaded.

AppRoutingModule

The AppRoutingModule is a module responsible for configuring and managing the routes of your application. It's part of the Angular Router, which allows you to define the navigation paths and associate them with specific components.

```typescript
import { NgModule } from '@angular/core';
import { RouterModule, Routes } from '@angular/router';
import { HomeComponent } from './components/home/home.component';
import { UserComponent } from './components/user/user.component';

const routes: Routes = [
  { path: '', component: HomeComponent, pathMatch: 'full' },
  { path: 'user', component: UserComponent, pathMatch: 'full' }
];

@NgModule({
  imports: [RouterModule.forRoot(routes)],
  exports: [RouterModule]
})
export class AppRoutingModule {}
```

In this example, we've defined 2 routes: one for the home component and one for the user component.

{path: '' }: This represents the default route or the root path. When the application is accessed without any specific route, the HomeComponent will be displayed. This is often used as the landing page or home page of the application.

{ path: 'user' }: This represents the route path '/user'. When the user navigates to '/user', the UserComponent will be displayed.

pathMatch: 'full': ensure that only a URL exactly matching '/user will trigger the redirection. Without pathMatch: 'full', any URL starting with '/user (e.g., '/user/some-route') would match, and the redirection would occur.

Navigation

To navigate between different views, you can use the routerLink directive in your templates or with Router service from code.

routerLink

The routerLink is a directive used for navigation in the application. It's used in the templates to create links that navigate to different views based on the defined routes. The routerLink directive can be applied to various HTML elements, such as <a>, <button>, or even custom components.

app.component.html

```html
<a routerLink="">Home</a>
<a routerLink="user">User</a>

<router-outlet></router-outlet>
```

Static Path: When the path is a static string, as in the example above, clicking the link or button will navigate to the specified route.

Dynamic Path: When the path is dynamic or depends on variables, you can use property binding with square brackets [].

```html
<a [routerLink]="['user',userId]">User</a>
```

If you want to capture a dynamic value for userId from the URL and pass it, use route configuration parameter.

```typescript
{ path: 'user/:userId', component: UserComponent }
```

user/:userId: This defines a route with a path segment 'user/' followed by a route parameter :userId. The colon : indicates that userId is a route parameter.

redirectTo

The redirectTo property is used to specify a redirection route when the current URL matches the path of the route. It's often used for setting up default routes or for redirecting users from one route to another.

```
const routes: Routes = [
  { path: '', pathMatch: 'full', redirectTo: '/users' },
  { path: 'users', pathMatch: 'full', component: UsersComponent }
];
```

If the current URL matches the path (which in this case is the root URL due to path: ''), Angular will redirect to the '/users' route.

Programmatic Navigation/Router

You can also navigate programmatically using the Router service. Programmatic navigation involves navigating from one view to another using TypeScript code rather than relying on user interactions with the UI.

The Angular Router is a powerful service that provides navigation capabilities for your Angular applications. It enables you to navigate between different views and components, manage application state, and handle route parameters and query parameters.

```
export class AppComponent {

  constructor(private router: Router) { }

  navigateToHome() {
    this.router.navigate(['/']); // Navigates to the root path
  }

  navigateToUser() {
    this.router.navigate(['/user', 1]); // Navigates to /user/1
  }

}
```

Query Parameters

Query parameters provide a way to pass optional data to a route. They are specified in the URL after a question mark (?) and can be accessed using the ActivatedRoute service.

```typescript
export class AppComponent {

  constructor(private router: Router) { }

  // Navigates to /user?userId=1
  navigateToUserWithQuery() {
    this.router.navigate(['/user'], { queryParams: { userId: 1 } });
  }
}
```

```typescript
export class UserComponent {

  constructor(private activatedRoute: ActivatedRoute) {}

  ngOnInit() {
    // Synchronous Way - Get userId from route
    const userId = this.activatedRoute.snapshot.queryParamMap.get('userId');

    // Asynchronous Way - Subscribe to the paramMap observable to react to
    // changes in route parameters
    this.activatedRoute.paramMap.subscribe(params => {
      // Get userId from route
      let userId = params.get('userId');
    });
  }
}
```

Use the synchronous method if you only need to access the route parameters once during the component initialization.

Use the asynchronous method if your component needs to react to changes in route parameters dynamically.

Route Segments

Route segments refer to the individual components of the route path separated by slashes ("/").
Each segment in the route path corresponds to a specific part of the route, allowing you to define
a hierarchical structure for your application.

```
const routes: Routes = [
  { path: 'user/:userId/:userRank', component: UserComponent }
];
```

Segment 1: 'user' is a static segment.

Segment 2: userId is the first dynamic segment, representing a user ID.

Segment 3: userRank is the second dynamic segment, representing a user rank or role.

```
import { Component } from "@angular/core";

export class UserComponent {

  constructor(private route: ActivatedRoute) { }

  ngOnInit() {
    // Extract route parameters from segments
    let userId = this.route.snapshot.params['userId'];
    let userRank = this.route.snapshot.params['userRank'];
  }
}
```

routerLinkActive

The routerLinkActive is a directive that allows you to apply a CSS class to an element when the associated route is active. It's useful for styling navigation links to provide visual feedback to users about the currently active route.

When the associated route is active, the specified CSS class (active in this case) will be applied to the element.

```html
<a routerLink="" routerLinkActive="active">Home</a>
<a routerLink="user" routerLinkActive="active">User</a>
```

```css
.active { color: red;}

.bold{ font-weight: bold; }
```

```html
<a routerLink="" routerLinkActive="active bold">Home</a>
```

You can also use routerLinkActive to apply multiple classes based on the current route

routerLinkActiveOptions

The routerLinkActiveOptions property is used in conjunction with the routerLinkActive directive to configure the behavior of the active CSS class application on a navigation link. This property allows you to fine-tune when the specified CSS classes should be applied based on the provided options.

```html
<a routerLink="/" routerLinkActive="active"
[routerLinkActiveOptions]="{exact: true}">Home</a>
```

exact (boolean):

[routerLinkActiveOptions]="{exact: true}": The exact: true option ensures that the classes are applied only when the route is exactly matched, the CSS class will be applied only if the router's URL is an exact match to the link's URL.

relativeTo (ActivatedRoute): Defines the base route for the link. This is useful when dealing with nested routes.

[routerLinkActiveOptions]="{relativeTo: someActivatedRoute}"

queryParams (string or string[]): Specifies one or more query parameters that must be present for the CSS class to be applied.

[routerLinkActiveOptions]="{queryParams: 'paramName'}"

fragment (string): Specifies the fragment that must be present for the CSS class to be applied.

[routerLinkActiveOptions]="{fragment: 'someFragment'}"

Path Wildcard

A path wildcard (**) is used to represent a wildcard or catch-all route. It matches any URL that doesn't match any of the defined routes. This wildcard route is often used for creating a default or fallback route, handling unknown routes, or implementing custom error handling

```
const routes: Routes = [
  { path: '', component: HomeComponent , pathMatch: 'full' },
  { path: 'user', component: UserComponent , pathMatch: 'full' },
  { path: '**', component: NotFoundComponent },
];
```

The wildcard route ('**') is defined at the end of the route configuration. It captures any URL that doesn't match any of the previous routes.

The wildcard route then redirects to a NotFoundComponent, which could be a custom component displaying a "Page Not Found" message.

Additional data associated with a route

You can provide additional data associated with a route using the data property in the route configuration. This data can be used for various purposes, such as setting page titles, meta tags, or any other information that is specific to a particular route.

```
const routes: Routes = [
  { path: 'user', component: UserComponent, data: { title: 'User' } }];
```

data: { title: 'User' }: This provides additional data for the route. In this case, it sets a 'title' property with the value 'User'.

```
export class UserComponent {
  constructor(private activatedRoute: ActivatedRoute) { }

  ngOnInit() {
    // Accessing route data
    let title = this.activatedRoute.snapshot.data['title'];
  }
}
```

Title

The title property sets the title of the page when this route is active.

```
const routes: Routes = [
  { path: '', component: HomeComponent, title: "Home" },
  { path: 'user', component: UserComponent, title: "User" }
];
```

Title service

The Title service is part of Angular's platform browser module and is used for manipulating the title of the HTML document

```
import { Title } from "@angular/platform-browser";

export class UserComponent {

  constructor(titleService: Title) {

    titleService.setTitle('New Page Title');
    const title = titleService.getTitle();
  }
}
```

Route children

When you have nested routes within a parent route, these are often referred to as "route children" or "child routes." Child routes allow you to organize and structure your application's routing in a hierarchical manner, making it more modular and maintainable.

```
const routes: Routes = [
  {
    path: 'user', component: UserComponent,
    children: [
      { path: 'add', component: UserAddComponent },
      { path: 'edit', component: UserEditComponent }
    ],
  }
];
```

The UserAddComponent is associated with the user/add route.

The UserEditComponent is associated with the user/edit route.

Fragment

A fragment is a part of the URL that comes after the '#' symbol. The fragment identifier is used to specify a certain section within the content of a document. For example, in the URL https://example.com/page#section1, #section1 is the fragment. When a user navigates to this URL, the browser will scroll to the section of the page with the corresponding id or name attribute equal to "section1". Fragments are commonly used to link directly to specific sections or elements within a single HTML page.

```
export class UserComponent {

  constructor(private router: Router) { }

  navigateToSection(section: string): void {

    // Navigate to the same route with a different fragment
    this.router.navigate(['/user', section], {fragment:`section-${section}`});

  }
}
```

```
<div id="section-users">Users Content</div>
<div id="section-add-user">Add User Content</div>
<div id="section-edit-user">Edit User Content</div>
```

When navigating to /user#section-add-user, it will scroll to the "Add User Content" in the UserComponent.

Route guards

Route guards are mechanisms to control navigation and access to routes. They allow you to execute code before a route is activated or when it's deactivated, enabling you to implement security, authentication, and other navigation-related logic. Angular provides several types of route guards:

CanActivate

Determines whether a route can be activated. It is commonly used for authentication purposes.

```
export const auth: CanActivateFn = (
  next: ActivatedRouteSnapshot,
  state: RouterStateSnapshot) => {
  let isAuth = false; // Your authentication logic here
  if (isAuth) {
    return true;
  } else {
    // Redirect to home page if not authenticated
    return inject(Router).createUrlTree([''])
  }
}

// Use canActivate
const routes: Routes = [
  { path: '', component: HomeComponent },
  { path: 'user', component: UserComponent, canActivate: [auth] },
];
```

auth: CanActivateFn defines a route guard function named auth that implements the CanActivateFn interface.

next: An ActivatedRouteSnapshot object representing the route about to be activated.

state: A RouterStateSnapshot object representing the current state of the router.

If the user is authenticated, the function returns true, allowing navigation to the protected route.

If not authenticated, it injects the Router service and returns a UrlTree that redirects to the home page ('').

CanActivateChild

CanActivateChild similar to CanActivate, but specifically for child routes.

```typescript
export const authChild: CanActivateChildFn = (
  childRoute: ActivatedRouteSnapshot,
  state: RouterStateSnapshot) => {
  let isAuth = false; // Your authentication logic here
  if (isAuth) {
    return true;
  } else {
    // Redirect to home page if not authenticated
    return inject(Router).createUrlTree([''])
  }
}

// Use canActivateChild
const routes: Routes = [
  { path: '', component: HomeComponent },
  { path: 'user', component: UserComponent, children: [
    { path: 'add', component: UserAddComponent,
                         canActivateChild: [authChild] }]
  }];
```

CanActivateChild Controls access to child routes, which are nested within parent routes.

Runs before activating each individual child route, allowing finer-grained control.

Useful for implementing specific permissions or restrictions on certain child routes within a broader parent area.

CanActivateChild allows you to create targeted safeguards for individual child routes based on additional criteria.

CanActivate vs CanActivateChild

Feature	CanActivate	CanActivateChild
Scope	Parent route and all its child routes	Individual child routes within a parent route
Execution order	Executed before any child route guards	Executed after parent CanActivate and before child CanActivate guards
Route data access	Accesses data for the parent route	Accesses data for both the parent and the child route

CanDeactivate

Determines whether a user can leave a route.

```
const canDeactivate: CanDeactivateFn<UserComponent> = (
  component: UserComponent,
  currentRoute: ActivatedRouteSnapshot,
  currentState: RouterStateSnapshot,
  nextState?: RouterStateSnapshot
) => {
  // return true if user can leave page in canLeave() function inside
  // UserComponent
  if (component.canLeave()) {
    return true; // Allow navigation
  }
   // Returns an Observable some custom dialog
   return this.dialogService.confirm('Navigate away?');
};

// Use canDeactive
const routes: Routes = [
  { path: 'user', component: UserComponent, canDeactivate: [canDeactivate]}
];
```

The CanDeactivate Guard is responsible for determining whether the user can navigate away from the 'user' route. It calls the canLeave() method of the UserComponent. If the method returns false, a confirmation dialog is displayed. This approach enables you to implement custom logic in the component to decide if the user should be allowed to leave the page.

CanMatch

CanMatch used to control whether a particular route can be matched during navigation.

```
const canMatch: CanMatchFn = (route: Route, segments: UrlSegment[]) => {
  // Extract the first segment from the URL
  const path = segments[0].path;

  // Define the allowed pattern (in this case, starting with "about")
  const allowedPattern = /^about/;

  // Return true if the URL matches the pattern, false otherwise
  return allowedPattern.test(path);
};

const routes: Routes = [
  { path: 'user', component: UserComponent, canMatch: [canMatch]}
];
```

The canMatch function takes two arguments:

route: The Route object associated with the current route.

segments: An array of UrlSegment objects representing the parts of the URL.

We extract the first segment's path (path) to check against the allowed pattern.

The allowedPattern regular expression matches URLs starting with "about".

The function returns true if the URL matches the pattern, indicating the user can access the route, otherwise it returns false.

CanMatch vs CanActivate

Feature	CanMatch	CanActivate
Execution order	Earlier, before component loading	Later, after component loading and before activation
Purpose	Lightweight permission checks	More complex logic, data fetching, authorization
Data access	No access to route data or activated component	Can access route data and activated component
Return value	Boolean	Boolean, Observable, or URLTree

Resolve

Performs data retrieval before route activation, useful for fetching data needed by a component.

```
const resolveUser: ResolveFn<User> = (route: ActivatedRouteSnapshot) => {

  const userId = route.paramMap.get('userId');
  return this.userService.getUser(userId); // Returns an Observable<User>

};

const routes: Routes = [
  { path: 'user', component: UserComponent, resolve: {user: resolveUser}}
];
```

```
export class UserComponent {

  constructor(private route: ActivatedRoute) {}

  ngOnInit() {
    this.route.data.subscribe(data => {
      const user = data['user']; // get the resolve user

    });
  }
}
```

The code demonstrates how to use a route resolver (resolveUser) to fetch user data before activating the 'user' route and how to access that resolved data within the UserComponent. This is useful when you need to ensure that certain data is available before rendering a component associated with a route.

Lazy loading

Lazy loading is a technique that allows you to load modules on-demand, rather than loading the entire application at once. This can significantly improve the initial loading time of your application because it only loads the necessary modules when the user navigates to a specific route. Angular provides a mechanism for lazy loading through the Angular Router.

```
const routes: Routes = [
  {
    path: 'lazy',
    loadChildren: () => import('./lazy/lazy.module').then(m => m.LazyModule)
  }
];
```

Component Lifecycle

Components go through a series of lifecycle events as they are created, rendered, and destroyed. These lifecycle events provide developers with hooks to execute code at specific points in the component's lifecycle. Understanding the Angular component lifecycle is crucial for performing tasks such as initializing data, handling DOM manipulation, and cleaning up resources.

Lifecycle Stage	Lifecycle Hooks	Description	When Called
Creation	Constructor	- Injects dependencies	When component is instantiated
	*ngOnInit	- Ideal for data fetching, setup tasks	After first change detection
Change Detection	None (automatic)	- Automatic checks for data/state changes	When relevant change occurs (e.g., user interaction, data subscription)
	markForCheck()	Manages change detection manually	Developer triggers manually
	detectChanges()	Manages change detection manually	Developer triggers manually
Data Updates	*ngOnChanges	Responds to input property changes	When input property changes
	*ngDoCheck	Runs after every change detection cycle (use cautiously)	After every change detection
Content & View Initialization	*ngAfterContentInit	Use after projected content (`<ng-content>`) initializes	After content initialization
	*ngAfterContentChecked	Use after content changes are checked	After content change detection
	*ngAfterViewInit	Use after component view initializes and is in DOM	After view initialization and insertion
	*ngAfterViewChecked	Use after view changes are checked	After view change detection
Destruction	*ngOnDestroy	Cleanup tasks like unsubscribing, releasing resources	Just before component is destroyed
		View removed from DOM	Memory is freed

Using OnInit hook:

```
import { OnInit } from "@angular/core";
export class UserComponent implements OnInit {

  ngOnInit() {

  }
}
```

The OnInit interface is used to implement the ngOnInit lifecycle hook in your component. The ngOnInit hook is called after the component has been initialized but before rendering.

However, it's not strictly necessary to explicitly implement the OnInit interface to use the ngOnInit lifecycle hook. Angular will still recognize and call the ngOnInit method even if you don't implement the interface. This is because Angular uses a mechanism called "duck typing," which checks for the presence of the method rather than requiring a specific interface implementation.

```
export class UserComponent {

  constructor() { console.log(1) }
  ngOnInit() { console.log(2) }
  ngOnChanges() { console.log('ngOnChanges') }
  ngDoCheck() { console.log(3) }
  ngAfterContentInit() { console.log(4) }
  ngAfterContentChecked() { console.log(5) }
  ngAfterViewInit() { console.log(6) }
  ngAfterViewChecked() { console.log(7) }
  ngOnDestroy() { console.log('ngOnDestroy') }

}
```

Change Detection

Angular's Change Detection mechanism is a core feature that allows the framework to efficiently update the view whenever there are changes in the application state. Change detection is the process by which Angular determines if and how the DOM should be updated to reflect the current state of the application. Here's an overview of how Angular's Change Detection works:

Initialization: When an Angular application is bootstrapped, Angular creates an initial view of the components and establishes a tree of change detectors. Each component has an associated change detector, responsible for tracking changes in the component and its children.

Change Detection Cycle: Angular operates on a zone-based change detection system. A zone is a execution context that allows Angular to intercept and track asynchronous tasks. The change detection cycle is triggered by various events, such as user actions, timers, HTTP requests, or other asynchronous tasks. During the change detection cycle, Angular runs change detection for all components starting from the root component.

Checking for Changes: For each component, Angular checks the component's properties, both those marked with @Input() and other properties that might be changed during the cycle. It compares the current and previous values of these properties. If there are differences, Angular marks the component and its ancestors as dirty.

Updating the View: After identifying the components that need to be updated, Angular updates the DOM to reflect the current state of the application. This process is known as the "render" phase.

Life Cycle Hooks: Angular provides lifecycle hooks such as ngOnChanges, ngOnInit, ngDoCheck, ngAfterContentInit, ngAfterViewInit, etc., which allow developers to execute custom logic at different points in the change detection cycle.

Immutable Data and Pure Pipes: Angular encourages the use of immutable data structures and pure pipes to optimize change detection. Immutable data ensures that objects are replaced rather than mutated, simplifying change detection checks.

Pure pipes only recalculate their result when the input data changes.

Performance Optimization: Angular employs various techniques for performance optimization, such as local change detection for components that don't have descendants, OnPush change detection strategy, and lazy loading.

Manual Control: Developers can manually trigger change detection using methods like markForCheck() and detectChanges() from the ChangeDetectorRef service.

Understanding the Angular Change Detection mechanism is crucial for building efficient and performant Angular applications. It's recommended to follow best practices, optimize data flow, and leverage Angular's features for better performance.

Trigger manually change detection

While Angular generally handles change detection automatically, there are cases where you might need to manually trigger it using markForCheck() or detectChanges().

markForCheck()

The markForCheck() is a method of the ChangeDetectorRef service in Angular. It's used to mark a component and its ancestors as dirty, which means Angular will check and update the component and its view during the next change detection cycle. This is particularly useful when dealing with scenarios where Angular's change detection may not be triggered automatically.

```typescript
import { ChangeDetectorRef } from '@angular/core';

export class UserComponent {

  constructor(private cdr: ChangeDetectorRef) { }

  myMethod() {
    // Do some work
    this.cdr.markForCheck(); // Mark the component for check
  }

}
```

In the example above, markForCheck() is called within a method of the component. It ensures that the component and its ancestors will be checked during the next change detection cycle, even if the change detection would not normally be triggered.

detectChanges()

The detectChanges() is a method of the Angular Change Detector itself. It forces the immediate execution of change detection for the component and its children. This method can be useful when you need to manually trigger change detection, for example, when dealing with asynchronous operations that Angular might not be aware of.

```typescript
import { ChangeDetectorRef } from '@angular/core';

export class UserComponent {

  constructor(private cdr: ChangeDetectorRef) {}

  myMethod() {
    // Do some work
    this.cdr.detectChanges(); // Manually trigger change detection
  }
}
```

In the example above, detectChanges() is called within a method of the component, causing the immediate execution of change detection. This method can be used in situations where you want to ensure that change detection happens immediately, bypassing the normal automatic change detection cycle.

NgZone

NgZone allow you to control whether code should run inside or outside the Angular zone.

NgZone helps manage and control the zones in which change detection runs. A zone is an execution context that includes a set of asynchronous tasks. NgZone provides a way to run code inside or outside of Angular's zone, which can be useful for optimizing performance and avoiding unnecessary change detection cycles.

```
export class UserComponent {

  constructor(private ngZone: NgZone) { }

  someAsyncOperation() {
    this.ngZone.run(() => {
      // Code to run inside Angular's zone
      // Change detection will be triggered after this code completes
    });

    this.ngZone.runOutsideAngular(() => {
      // Code to run outside Angular's zone
      // Change detection will not be triggered after this code completes
    });
  }
}
```

Http Package

Http is an Angular package that contains the HttpClient service and other supporting services and features for making HTTP requests in Angular applications.

HttpClient

By using provideHttpClient(), you ensure that HttpClient is available throughout your application with the default XMLHttpRequest.

```
import { provideHttpClient} from '@angular/common/http';

@NgModule({
  providers: [provideHttpClient()],
  imports: []
})
export class AppModule { }
```

HttpClient is a service for making HTTP requests. The HttpClient simplifies the process of interacting with RESTful APIs or fetching data from servers.

```
export class UserComponent {
  constructor(private httpClient: HttpClient) {

    const apiUrl = 'https://api.eldar.com/getUsers';

    httpClient.get(apiUrl)
      .subscribe({
        next: (data: any) => {
          console.log(data);},
        error: (error) => {
          console.error(error);},
        complete: () => {
          console.log('Request complete');}
      });
  }
}
```

HttpClient support methods:
httpClient.
- delete
- get
- head
- jsonp
- options
- patch
- post
- put
- request

The subscribe method is used to subscribe to the observable returned by the get method. It takes an object with two properties:

next: This callback is called when a successful response is received. In this case, it logs the data to the console using console.log(data).

error: This callback is called if there is an error during the HTTP request. It logs the error to the console using console.error(error).

complete: This callback is called regardless of whether it was successful or encountered an error.

The use of subscribe is essential because Angular's HTTP methods return observables. Observables are a part of the reactive programming paradigm and provide a way to handle asynchronous operations, such as HTTP requests. The subscribe method allows you to define what happens when the observable emits values (success) or encounters an error.

If you want to customize the behavior of the HTTP client. For example, withFetch might enable you to use the Fetch API under the hood instead of the default XMLHttpRequest.

provideHttpClient(withFetch()): This replaces the default Angular HttpClient implementation with a version that uses the browser's built-in fetch API instead of the older, less browser-compatible XMLHttpRequest (XHR) API. This can offer performance and flexibility benefits in modern browsers.

```
import { provideHttpClient, withFetch } from '@angular/common/http';

@NgModule({
    provideHttpClient(withFetch()),
)],
  imports: []
})
export class AppModule { }
```

Interceptors

Interceptors are a way to intercept HTTP requests and responses globally before they reach the application or after they leave it. Interceptors provide a way to modify or inspect the HTTP request or response, add custom headers, handle errors, or perform other tasks. They are implemented as classes that implement the HttpInterceptor interface.

```
import { HTTP_INTERCEPTORS, provideHttpClient, withFetch } from
'@angular/common/http';

@NgModule({
  providers: [
  {
    provide: HTTP_INTERCEPTORS, useClass: RequestInterceptor, multi: true },
    provideHttpClient(withFetch(), withInterceptorsFromDi()),
  ],
  imports: []
})
export class AppModule { }
```

{ provide: HTTP_INTERCEPTORS, useClass: RequestInterceptor, multi: true }: This configures Angular to use an HTTP_INTERCEPTOR named RequestInterceptor. The multi: true flag allows multiple interceptors to be used in a chain.

withInterceptorsFromDi(): When you include withInterceptorsFromDi() in the provideHttpClient configuration, Angular will automatically include all interceptors that are provided via the HTTP_INTERCEPTORS token in the DI system.

Request Interceptor

```typescript
import { HttpClient, HttpEvent, HttpHandler, HttpInterceptor, HttpRequest } from
"@angular/common/http";
import { Injectable } from "@angular/core";

@Injectable()
export class RequestInterceptor implements HttpInterceptor {

  intercept(req: HttpRequest<any>, next: HttpHandler):
    Observable<HttpEvent<any>> {

    // Add a custom header to the request
    const modifiedRequest = request.clone({
          headers: request.headers.append('X-Custom-Header', 'CustomValue'),
    });
    return next.handle(modifiedRequest);
  }
}
```

intercept Method: This method is required to be implemented as part of the HttpInterceptor interface. It takes two parameters:

req: The original HttpRequest being intercepted.

next: The HttpHandler that will process the modified request.

The method returns an Observable<HttpEvent<any>>, indicating that it will handle HTTP events and potentially modify the request.

Modifying the Request: The clone method is used to create a copy of the original request (req). The headers property is used to specify the HTTP headers for an HTTP request. We are adding a custom header to the request's headers. The request.headers.append() method is used to create a new instance of the HttpHeaders object with the specified header appended to it. In this example, a custom header 'X-Custom-Header' with the value 'CustomValue' is added to the request.

Returning the Modified Request: The modified request is passed to next.handle() to allow it to continue through the HTTP request chain. The interceptor returns the Observable<HttpEvent<any>>, indicating that it has completed its interception.

By using this interceptor, any HTTP request made in your Angular application will have the custom header 'X-Custom-Header: CustomValue' added to it.

withCredentials

By default, when you make an HTTP request using Angular's HttpClient module, the browser does not include cookies or HTTP authentication credentials (such as HTTP authentication headers) in the request if the request is cross-origin. This behavior is a security feature implemented by browsers to prevent unauthorized access to sensitive information.

The withCredentials option is used when making HTTP requests to specify whether cookies and other credentials should be sent along with the request.

In this example, the fetchData method makes an HTTP GET request to https://example.com/api/data and includes credentials in the request by setting the withCredentials option to true.

```
fetchData() {
    this.http.get('https://site.com/api/data', { withCredentials: true });
}
```

In this example we set the withCredentials property to true globally for all HTTP requests:

```
@Injectable()
export class HttpRequestInterceptor implements HttpInterceptor {

    constructor(private cookieService: CookieService) { }

    intercept(request: HttpRequest<any>, next: HttpHandler): Observable<HttpEvent<any>> {

        const modifiedRequest = request.clone({
            withCredentials: true
        });

        return next.handle(modifiedRequest).pipe();
    }
}
```

Response Interceptor

```typescript
import { HttpClient, HttpErrorResponse, HttpEvent, HttpHandler,
HttpInterceptor, HttpRequest, HttpResponse } from "@angular/common/http";
import { Injectable } from "@angular/core";

@Injectable()
export class ResponseInterceptor implements HttpInterceptor {
  intercept(request: HttpRequest<any>, next: HttpHandler):
Observable<HttpEvent<any>> {
    return next.handle(request).pipe(
      tap((event: HttpEvent<any>) => {
        if (event instanceof HttpResponse) {
          // Check the status code in the response
          console.log('Response status code:', event.status);

          // You can perform actions based on the status code
          if (event.status === 401) {   }
        }
      }),
      catchError((error: HttpErrorResponse) => {
        // Handle HTTP errors
        console.error('HTTP Error:', error);

        // Pass the error along to be handled by the subscriber
        return throwError(() => error);
      })
    );
  }
}
```

next.handle(request) method: allows the request to proceed through the request chain.

pipe function: Used to chain operators to the observable returned by next.handle(request).

tap operator: is used to perform actions on the observable sequence, specifically when an HttpResponse event is encountered. In this example, it logs the response status code and checks if it's 401 (Unauthorized), allowing you to perform custom actions based on the status code.

catchError operator: is used to catch any HTTP errors that may occur during the request.

It logs the error and passes it along to be handled by the subscriber using throwError(() => error).

Forms

Angular's forms module enables the creation of dynamic and interactive forms using either Template-Driven Forms or Reactive Forms.

Template-Driven Forms

Template-Driven Forms are based on directives in the template and are generally less code-intensive.

```html
<form #myForm="ngForm" (ngSubmit)="onSubmit(myForm)">
    <br>
    <input type="email" name="email" ngModel>
    <br>
    <input type="text" name="fullName" ngModel>
    <br>
    <button type="submit">Submit</button>
</form>
```

```
mail
Eldar Cohen
Submit
```

```typescript
import { NgForm } from "@angular/forms";

export class UserComponent {

  onSubmit(form: NgForm) {
      console.log(form.value); // {email: 'mail', fullName: 'Eldar Cohen'}
      form.resetForm()
  }
}
```

#myForm="ngForm": Creates a reference to the form using the template reference variable #myForm and associates it with the ngForm directive.

(ngSubmit)="onSubmit(myForm)": Binds the ngSubmit event to the onSubmit method in your component when the form is submitted.

<input> name attributes: Used to identify form controls when the form is submitted.

<input> ngModel attributes: used for two-way data binding, connecting the form controls to the underlying data in your component.

When the form is submitted, the onSubmit method in your component will be called, passing the form reference (myForm) as an argument.

form.resetForm(): clear the values of an existing form

Validations

Handle form validations with Template-Driven Forms.

```html
<form #myForm="ngForm" (ngSubmit)="onSubmit(myForm)" novalidate>
    <br>
    <input type="email" name="email" ngModel required email>
    <br>
    <input type="text" name="fullName" ngModel minlength="2" maxlength="50">
    <br>
    <input type="number" name="age" ngModel min="18" max="67">
    <br>
    Is Form Valid: {{myForm.valid}}
    <br>
    <button type="submit">Submit</button>
</form>
```

```typescript
export class UserComponent {

  onSubmit(form: NgForm) {
    if (form.valid) {

    }
  }
}
```

Is Form Valid: false

Submit

novalidate: Used on form element to disable browser native validation.

Angular validation directives: required, email, minlength, maxlength, min, and max are used to apply validation rules.

form.valid: Inside onSubmit we check to determine if the form is valid.

When the user submits the form, the onSubmit method is called, and it checks whether the form is valid before performing any further actions. The validity of the form is displayed in the template using {{myForm.valid}}.

90

Custom error messages to each field

```html
<form #myForm="ngForm" (ngSubmit)="onSubmit(myForm)" novalidate>
    <input type="email" name="email" #email="ngModel"
                        [(ngModel)]="model.email" required email>
    <div *ngIf="email.errors && (email.dirty || email.touched)">
        <div *ngIf="email.errors['required']">required</div>
        <div *ngIf="email.errors['email']">email format invalid</div>
    </div>
    <br>
    <input type="text" name="fullName" #fullName="ngModel"
            [(ngModel)]="model.fullName" minlength="2" maxlength="50">
    <div *ngIf="fullName.errors && (fullName.dirty || fullName.touched)">
        <div *ngIf="fullName.errors['minlength']">min length 2</div>
        <div *ngIf="fullName.errors['maxlength']">max length 50</div>
    </div>
    <br>
    <input type="number" name="age" #age="ngModel"
                        [(ngModel)]="model.age" min="18" max="67">
    <div *ngIf="age.errors && (age.dirty || age.touched || age.pristine)">
        <div *ngIf="age.errors['min']">min value 18</div>
        <div *ngIf="age.errors['max']">max value 67</div>
    </div>

    <br>
    <button type="submit">Submit</button>
</form>
```

```typescript
export class UserComponent {

  model = {
    email: '',
    fullName: '',
    age: 0
  }
  onSubmit(form: NgForm) {
    if (form.valid) {

    }
  }
}
```

91

Creates a template reference variable: Associated with the ngModel directive, allowing you to access the NgModel instance for the input, #email="ngModel", #fullName="ngModel", #age="ngModel".

Two-way data binding: Binds the input value to the model property in your component, [(ngModel)]="model.email", [(ngModel)]="model.fullName", [(ngModel)]="model.age".

*ngIf: directive to conditionally display error messages only when the input has errors and has been interacted with (dirty or touched or pristine) and specific error messages based on the type of error (required, email, minlength, maxlength, min, and max).

Dirty: The "dirty" state refers to the condition where the user has interacted with a form control, making it "dirty." For an input field, it becomes dirty when the user types or modifies its content. The dirty property in Angular is a boolean property that is true if the control has been interacted with, and its value has changed since it was initialized.

Touched: The "touched" state indicates whether a form control has lost focus after being interacted with. For an input field, it becomes touched when the user clicks into the field, modifies its content, and then clicks away, causing the field to lose focus. The touched property in Angular is a boolean property that is true if the control has been touched (lost focus) at least once.

Pristine: The "pristine" state is the opposite of "dirty." A form control is considered pristine if the user has not interacted with it. For an input field, it is pristine when it has not been modified or focused since it was initialized. The pristine property in Angular is a boolean property that is true if the control has not been touched or modified.

[ ]	[3f3]	[eldar@g.com]
required	email format invalid	[Eldar Cohen]
[5]		[30]
min length 2	[12]	[Submit]
[15]	[99]	
min value 18	max value 67	
[Submit]	[Submit]	

Reactive Forms

Reactive Forms are more code-driven and provide a reactive approach to handling forms. They are built using FormBuilder service to create FormGroup and FormControl instances.

Add ReactiveFormsModule to app module:

```
@NgModule({
  imports: [
    FormsModule,
    ReactiveFormsModule
  ]
})
import { FormBuilder, FormGroup, Validators } from "@angular/forms";

export class UserComponent {
  form: FormGroup;

  constructor(private fb: FormBuilder) {
    this.form = this.fb.group({
      // Define your form controls with initial values and validators
      email: ['mail@g.com', [Validators.required, Validators.email]],
      fullName: ['', [Validators.minLength(2), Validators.maxLength(50)]],
      age: ['', [Validators.min(18), Validators.min(67)]]
    });
  }

  onSubmit() {
    if (this.form.valid) {
      console.log(this.form.value);
      this.form.reset();
    }
  }
}
```

form: FormGroup: This declares a property form of type FormGroup to hold the entire form.

this.form = this.fb.group({ ... }): It initializes the form using FormBuilder. Inside the group method, you define the form controls (email, fullName, and age) with their initial values and associated validators.

this.form.reset(): clear the values of an existing form

```
<form [formGroup]="form" (ngSubmit)="onSubmit()">
    <input type="email" formControlName="email">
    <div *ngIf="form.get('email')!.errors &&
                (form.get('email')!.dirty || form.get('email')!.touched)">
      <div *ngIf="form.get('email')!.errors!['required']">required</div>
      <div *ngIf="form.get('email')!.errors!['email']">
                                        email format invalid</div>
    </div>
    <br>
    <input type="text" formControlName="fullName">
    <div *ngIf="form.get('fullName')!.errors &&
          (form.get('fullName')!.dirty || form.get('fullName')!.touched)">
      <div *ngIf="form.get('fullName')!.errors!['minlength']">
                                        min length 2</div>
      <div *ngIf="form.get('fullName')!.errors!['maxlength']">
                                        max length 50</div>
    </div>
    <br>
    <input type="number" formControlName="age">
    <div
        *ngIf="form.get('age')!.errors && (form.get('age')!.dirty ||
                    form.get('age')!.touched || form.get('age')!.pristine)">
      <div *ngIf="form.get('age')!.errors!['min']">min value 18</div>
      <div *ngIf="form.get('age')!.errors!['max']">max value 67</div>
    </div>

    <br>
    <button type="submit">Submit</button>
</form>
```

[formGroup]="form": This binds the form property from the component to the form in the template.

formControlName: Each input field is associated with a form control using formControlName. Validation messages are displayed conditionally based on the state of the form control (e.g., dirty, touched, pristine).

form.get(): The method is a part of the Angular Reactive Forms module, and it is used to retrieve a reference to a specific form control within a FormGroup.

Custom validator – Reactive Forms

Custom validators are functions that you can create to add custom validation logic to your reactive forms. These validators are used to validate the input value of a form control based on your specific requirements.

```typescript
import { AbstractControl, ValidationErrors } from '@angular/forms';

export function isUpperCaseValidator(control: AbstractControl):
ValidationErrors | null {
  if (!(control.value && /^[A-Z]/.test(control.value))) {
    return { isUpperCase: true }; // fail
  }
  return null; // pass
}
```

The isUpperCaseValidator defines a function which takes an AbstractControl (representing the form control to be validated) as a parameter. It returns either a ValidationErrors object if the validation fails or null if the validation passes.

if (!(control.value && /^[A-Z]/.test(control.value))): This line checks if the control's value is not empty and does not start with an uppercase letter. The regular expression /^[A-Z]/ checks if the value starts with an uppercase letter.

return { isUpperCase: true }: If the validation fails, it returns a ValidationErrors object with a property isUpperCase set to true. This indicates that the validation has failed.

return null: If the validation passes, it returns null, indicating that there are no validation errors.

```typescript
export class UserComponent {
  form: FormGroup;

  constructor(private fb: FormBuilder) {
    this.form = this.fb.group({
      fullName: ['', [isUpperCaseValidator]],
    });
  }

  onSubmit() {
    if (this.form.valid) { }
  }
}
```

this.form = this.fb.group({ fullName: ['', [isUpperCaseValidator]], }): Inside the constructor, it uses the FormBuilder to create a form named form. The form has a single control named fullName with an initial value of an empty string (''). Additionally, it applies the custom validator isUpperCaseValidator to the fullName control. This means that the form will be considered invalid if the fullName control does not start with an uppercase letter.

```html
<form [formGroup]="form" (ngSubmit)="onSubmit()">
    <br>
    <input type="text" formControlName="fullName">
    <div *ngIf="form.get('fullName')!.errors!['isUpperCase']">
    String must start with Capital letter
    </div>
    <br>
    <button type="submit">Submit</button>
</form>
```

<div *ngIf="form.get('fullName')!.errors!['isUpperCase']">: This line uses the *ngIf directive to conditionally render a <div> element. It checks if the isUpperCase error exists in the errors property of the fullName control. If the error is present, the message "String must start with Capital letter" will be displayed.

Custom validator – Template-Driven Forms

```typescript
import { Directive } from "@angular/core";
import { AbstractControl,NG_VALIDATORS, ValidationErrors, Validator } from
"@angular/forms";
@Directive({
  selector: '[isUpperCase]',
  providers: [ { provide: NG_VALIDATORS, useExisting:UpperCaseDirective,
                 multi: true,} ],
  standalone: true,
})
export class UpperCaseDirective implements Validator {
  validate(control: AbstractControl): ValidationErrors | null {
    if (!(control.value && /^[A-Z]/.test(control.value))) {
      return { isUpperCase: true }; // fail
    }
    return null; // pass
  }
}
```

selector: '[isUpperCase]': Specifies that this directive can be used in the template with the attribute isUpperCase.

providers: Configures the injector to provide instances of this directive and the NG_VALIDATORS token. It uses the UpperCaseDirective as the implementation and sets multi: true to allow multiple validators.

standalone: true: Indicates that this directive should not be part of a larger directive or component. It is a standalone directive.

validate: The validate method takes an AbstractControl as a parameter, representing the form control to be validated. It checks if the control's value exists and starts with an uppercase letter using a regular expression (/^[A-Z]/).

If the validation fails (value is either empty or doesn't start with an uppercase letter), it returns a validation error object with the key isUpperCase set to true. Otherwise, it returns null to indicate a successful validation.

```
<form #myForm="ngForm" (ngSubmit)="onSubmit(myForm)">
    <br>
    <input type="email" name="email" ngModel isUpperCase>
    <br>
    <button type="submit">Submit</button>
</form>
```

isUpperCase: Using the custom UpperCaseDirective.

Async Custom validator – Reactive Forms

Asynchronous custom validators are useful when you need to perform asynchronous operations, such as making an HTTP request or working with a timeout. Async validators are typically used to check values against a server or perform other asynchronous tasks.

```
import { AbstractControl, ValidationErrors, AsyncValidator } from
'@angular/forms';
import { Observable, catchError, map, of } from "rxjs";
export class EmailOccupiedValidator implements AsyncValidator {
  constructor(private emailService: EmailService) { }
  validate(control: AbstractControl): Observable<ValidationErrors | null> {
    return this.emailService.isEmailOccupied(control.value).pipe(
      map((isTaken) => (isTaken ? { emailOccupied: true } : null)),
      catchError(() => of(null)),);
  }
}
```

EmailOccupiedValidator implements AsyncValidator: This line defines the EmailOccupiedValidator class, which implements the AsyncValidator interface. The AsyncValidator interface requires the implementation of a validate method.

EmailService: The EmailService provide a method named isEmailOccupied for checking whether an email is already occupied or in use.

validate(control: AbstractControl): This method is required by the AsyncValidator interface. It takes an AbstractControl (representing the form control being validated) and returns an Observable of type ValidationErrors or null. The use of Observable indicates that the validation process is asynchronous, and the result will be emitted over time.

return this.emailService.isEmailOccupied(control.value).pipe(: This line calls the isEmailOccupied method of the injected EmailService. The method returns an observable indicating whether the email is occupied.

map((isTaken) => (isTaken ? { emailOccupied: true } : null)): The result from the isEmailOccupied method is processed using the map operator. If the email is taken, it returns a ValidationErrors object with the emailOccupied property set to true. If the email is not taken, it returns null.

catchError(() => of(null)): The catchError operator is used to handle any errors that might occur during the asynchronous validation process. In this case, if an error occurs, it returns of(null), indicating that the validation should pass.

```
export class UserComponent {
  form: FormGroup;

  constructor(private fb: FormBuilder) {
    this.form = this.fb.group({
      fullName: ['', null, [EmailOccupiedValidator]],
    });
  }
}
```

In the this.fb.group method, the third parameter is meant for asynchronous validators, and it should be an array of asynchronous validators.

Async Custom validator – Template-Driven Forms

```
import {Directive, forwardRef } from "@angular/core";
import { AbstractControl, AsyncValidator, NG_ASYNC_VALIDATORS,
ValidationErrors, Validator } from "@angular/forms";
import { Observable, catchError, map, of } from "rxjs";

@Directive({
  selector: '[emailOccupied]',
  providers: [
    {
      provide: NG_ASYNC_VALIDATORS,
      useExisting: forwardRef(() => EmailOccupiedDirective),
      multi: true,
    },
  ],
  standalone: true,
})
export class EmailOccupiedDirective implements AsyncValidator {
  validate(control: AbstractControl): Observable<ValidationErrors | null> {
    const email = control.value;
    return this.emailService.isEmailOccupied(email).pipe(
      map((isOccupied) => (isOccupied ? { emailOccupied: true } : null)),
      catchError(() => of(null)));
  }
}
```

providers: The NG_ASYNC_VALIDATORS: This indicates that the class implements asynchronous validation and should be registered as an asynchronous validator.

validate(control: AbstractControl): This method takes an AbstractControl (representing the form control being validated) and returns an observable of type ValidationErrors or null. It performs asynchronous validation logic by calling isEmailOccupied on emailService.

```
<form #myForm="ngForm" (ngSubmit)="onSubmit(myForm)">
    <br>
    <input type="email" name="email" ngModel emailOccupied >
    <br>
    <button type="submit">Submit</button>
</form>
```

emailOccupied: Using the custom EmailOccupiedDirective.

Control Value Accessor

If you create a custom form control like component, you need to ensure it can work with Angular's form system. This is where ControlValueAccessor comes in.

ControlValueAccessor allows to send/get values to/from the control.

Implement ControlValueAccessor: You create methods to handle value changes and state updates.

Register Your Custom Control: Use NG_VALUE_ACCESSOR to tell Angular about your custom control and how to use it with forms.

```typescript
import { Component, forwardRef } from '@angular/core';
import { ControlValueAccessor, NG_VALUE_ACCESSOR } from '@angular/forms';

@Component({
  selector: 'app-custom-dropdown',
  template: `<select [value]="value" (change)="onChange($event)">
            <option *ngFor="let option of options" [value]="option">{{ option }}</option>
            </select>`,
  providers: [{ provide: NG_VALUE_ACCESSOR,
      useExisting: forwardRef(() => CustomDropdownComponent),
      multi: true}]
})
export class CustomDropdownComponent implements ControlValueAccessor {
  value: any = '';
  options = ['Option 1', 'Option 2', 'Option 3'];

  //Callback function to be called when the control is touched (focused and blurred)
  onTouched: () => void = () => { };
  onChange = (value: any) => { };

  //init value in form.
  writeValue(value: any): void { this.value = value; }
  // set the result
  setValue(val) { this.onChange(val); }

  //Angular calls this method to register a function that should be called when the
  //control's value changes.
```

```
  registerOnChange(fn: (value: any) => void): void { this.onChange = fn; }


  //Angular calls this method to register a function that should be called when the control
  //is touched.
  registerOnTouched(fn: () => void): void { this.onTouched = fn; }


  //Called by Angular to enable or disable the control
  setDisabledState?(isDisabled: boolean): void {
    // Example: this.element.nativeElement.disabled = isDisabled;
  }
}
```

The two most important functions when implementing ControlValueAccessor are:

writeValue: Initializes the control with value.

onChange: Propagates the value back to the form when the control changes.

```
<form [formGroup]="myForm">
  <app-custom-dropdown formControlName="myDropdown"></app-custom-dropdown>
</form>
```

```
@Component({ selector: 'app-my-form', templateUrl: './my-form.component.html'})
export class MyFormComponent  {
  myForm: FormGroup;

  constructor( private fb: FormBuilder){
    this.myForm = this.fb.group({
      myDropdown: ['Option 2'] // This will trigger writeValue() with 'Option 2'
    });
  }
  // Method to programmatically set the value of the custom dropdown
  setDropdownValue() {
    this.myForm.get('myDropdown')?.setValue('Option 3');
    // This triggers writeValue() in the custom component
  }


  // Method to get the current value of the custom dropdown from onChange
  getDropdownValue() {
    const currentValue = this.myForm.get('myDropdown')?.value;
    // Access the value from the FormControl
  }
}
```

Add Scripts and Styles

You can add scripts and styles to your application in several ways.

index.html

Open the src/index.html file.

Add the script tags directly within the html.

```html
<head>
  <link rel="stylesheet" href="style.css">
</head>
<body>
  <app-root></app-root>
  <script src="script.js"></script>
</body>
</html>
```

angular.json

Open your angular.json file.

Locate the styles array under the build or test options, and add the paths to your style files.

```json
"projects": {
  "your-app-name": {
    "architect": {
      "build": {
        "options": {
          "styles": [ "src/styles.less", // Add more style paths],
          "scripts": [ "src/script.js", // Add more scripts paths]
        }
      }
    }
  }
}
```

Add Assets

To add assets to your Angular application, Use the assets configuration in the angular.json file. This allows you to include files like images, fonts, or other static resources that your application needs.

```json
"projects": {
  "your-app-name": {
    "architect": {
      "build": {
        "options": {
          "assets": ["src/assets", "src/favicon.ico",//Add more asset paths]
        }
      }
    }
  }
}
```

Environments

You can use environments folder to store environment-specific configuration files. These files help manage different settings, such as API endpoints, feature flags, or any other configuration that may vary between development, testing, and production environments.

Create environments folder with environment files:

environment.ts

```typescript
export const environment = {
  apiUrl: 'http://localhost:3000',
  isProd: false
};
```

environment.ts

```typescript
export const environment = {
  apiUrl: 'http://api.eldar.com',
  isProd: true
};
```

Add paths to angular.json file in production section:

```json
"configurations": {
  "production": {
    "fileReplacements": [
      {
        "replace": "src/environments/environment.ts",
        "with": "src/environments/environment.prod.ts"
      }]
  }
}
```

Use environment file:

```typescript
import { environment } from "../../../environments/environment";

export class UserComponent {
  constructor() {
    let url = environment.apiUrl;
  }
}
```

Production

Use the Angular CLI to build the production version of your application:

```
ng build --configuration production
```

Libraries

Angular has a vibrant ecosystem with a variety of third-party libraries that can enhance and simplify development tasks.

npm-check

The npm-check is a useful command-line tool for checking the status of your npm project dependencies. It allows you to see which of your project's dependencies are out-of-date, which ones have updates available, and provides an interactive interface to selectively update them.

Install command: `npm install -g npm-check`

npm-check -gu

npm-check -gu: Interactively update global npm packages to their latest versions.

-g: Checks for global packages.

-u: Updates outdated packages interactively.

```
Minor Update New backwards-compatible features.
>( ) npm           10.2.5  >  10.4.0  https://docs.npmjs.com/
 ( ) @angular/cli  17.0.8  >  17.1.3  https://github.com/angular/angular-cli

Space to select. Enter to start upgrading. Control-C to cancel.
```

npm-check -u

npm-check -u: Interactively update local npm packages inside current project to their latest versions.

```
? Choose which packages to update. (Press <space> to select, <a> to toggle all, <i> to invert selection)

Patch Update Backwards-compatible bug fixes.
>( ) jasmine-core devDep  5.1.1  >  5.1.2  https://jasmine.github.io

Minor Update New backwards-compatible features.
 ( ) @angular/animations          17.0.8  >  17.1.3  https://github.com/angular/angular#readme
 ( ) @angular/common              17.0.8  >  17.1.3  https://github.com/angular/angular#readme
 ( ) @angular/compiler            17.0.8  >  17.1.3  https://github.com/angular/angular#readme
 ( ) @angular/core                17.0.8  >  17.1.3  https://github.com/angular/angular#readme
 ( ) @angular/forms               17.0.8  >  17.1.3  https://github.com/angular/angular#readme
(Move up and down to reveal more choices)
```

ngx-cookie-service

The ngx-cookie-service is a library that provides a service for handling cookies in Angular applications. Cookies are small pieces of data stored on the client-side (in the user's browser) and are commonly used for various purposes, such as session management, user authentication, and tracking user behavior. The ngx-cookie-service library simplifies the process of working with cookies in Angular applications by providing a convenient Angular service to interact with them.

Install: `npm install ngx-cookie-service`

```
import { CookieService } from 'ngx-cookie-service';

class MyComponent {
    constructor(private cookieService: CookieService) {

        // Setting a Cookie:
        cookieService.set('cookieName', 'cookieValue');

        // Getting a Cookie:
        const cookieValue = cookieService.get('cookieName');

        // Checking if a Cookie Exists:
        const cookieExists = cookieService.check('cookieName');

        // Deleting a Cookie:
        cookieService.delete('cookieName');

    }
}
```

ngx-translate

The ngx-translate library is an internationalization (i18n) library that's help to manage translations and handle multilingual content in Angular projects.

Install: `npm ngx-translate/core`

Configure the TranslateModule in your Angular module:

```typescript
import { HttpClient, provideHttpClient, withFetch } from
'@angular/common/http';
import { TranslateLoader, TranslateModule } from '@ngx-translate/core';
import { TranslateHttpLoader } from '@ngx-translate/http-loader';

@NgModule({
  imports: [
    TranslateModule.forRoot({
      loader: {
        provide: TranslateLoader,
        useFactory: (createTranslateLoader),
        deps: [HttpClient]
      }
    }),
  ],
  providers: [provideHttpClient(withFetch())],
})
export class AppModule { }

export function createTranslateLoader(http: HttpClient) {
  return new TranslateHttpLoader(http,'./assets/i18n/', '.json');
}
```

The createTranslateLoader function is defined to return a new instance of TranslateHttpLoader. This loader is configured to fetch translations from JSON files located in the ./assets/i18n/ directory.

Create json files in the directory ./assets/i18n/ :

en.json

```json
{
  "hello": "Hello",
  "english": "English",
}
```

he.json

```json
{
  "hello": "שלום",
  "english": "אנגלית",
}
```

Use the TranslateService in your component:

```typescript
import { TranslateService } from '@ngx-translate/core';

class MyClass {
    constructor(private translate: TranslateService) {

        // Setting Default Language
        translate.setDefaultLang('he');

        //Switching Language
        this.translate.use('en');

        //Synchronous Fetching and Using Translations
        const str = this.translate.instant('hello');

        //Asynchronous Fetching and Using Translations
        this.translate.get(['hello'])
            .subscribe(translations => {
                const str = translations['hello'];
            });

        //Get Current Language
        const currentLang = this.translate.currentLang;

    }
}
```

The translate.get() is used to fetch translations asynchronously for the key 'hello'. When the translations are available, the subscribe() method is called to access the translations. Inside the subscription callback, the translation for the 'hello' key is retrieved from the translations object.

```
this.translate.stream(['hello']).subscribe(translations => {
        const str = translations['hello'];
});
```

Similarly, translate.stream() is used to fetch translations asynchronously for the key 'hello'. This method also returns an Observable that emits the translations when they are available. The subscribe() method is called to access the translations, and inside the subscription callback, the translation for the 'hello' key is retrieved from the translations object.

Both approaches achieve the same result of asynchronously fetching translations for the 'hello' key. The difference lies in how they handle the fetching mechanism:

translate.get() retrieves translations once when called and emits them immediately.

translate.stream() provides translations as an Observable stream, which means it can emit multiple times if translations change dynamically.

Use the translate pipe in your templates:

```
{{'hello' | translate}}
```

Angular Material

Angular Material is a UI component library for Angular applications. It provides a set of pre-built and customizable UI components that follow the Material Design guidelines, helping developers create visually appealing and consistent user interfaces.

Material Design Components: Angular Material includes a wide range of Material Design components such as buttons, cards, dialogs, tabs, forms, and more.

Theming: It supports theming to allow developers to easily customize the appearance of their application. You can define your color palette, typography, and other styles.

Responsive Design: The components are designed to be responsive and work well on different screen sizes and devices.

Animation: It includes built-in support for Angular animations, enabling developers to create smooth and interactive user interfaces.

Install:

```
npm i @angular/material
```

```
npm i @angular/cdk
```

MatDialog

MatDialog is a part of Angular Material and is used to create modal dialogs (pop-up windows). Modal dialogs are commonly used for tasks such as displaying forms, confirmation messages, or other temporary content that requires user interaction.

In your module file, import MatDialogModule and OverlayModule.

Include Material Design styles:

In the component file @import '~@angular/material/prebuilt-themes/indigo-pink.css';

Or add the path to angular.json file, section style, "node_modules/@angular/material/prebuilt-themes/indigo-pink.css"

```
export class DialogData {
  title?: string;
  content?: string;
}
```

```
import { Component, Inject } from '@angular/core';

@Component({
  selector: 'my-dialog-content',
  template: `<h1 mat-dialog-title>{{ data.title }}</h1>
             <div mat-dialog-content>
               {{ data.content }}
             </div>
             <div mat-dialog-actions>
              <button mat-button (click)="onNoClick()">Close</button>
             </div>`
})
export class MyDialogContentComponent {
  constructor(
    public dialogRef: MatDialogRef<MyDialogContentComponent>,
    @Inject(MAT_DIALOG_DATA) public data: DialogData) {}

  onNoClick(): void {
    this.dialogRef.close();
  }
}
```

```
import { MatDialog } from '@angular/material/dialog';
import { MyDialogContentComponent } from './my-dialog-content.component';

@Component({
  selector: 'my-component',
  template: `<button mat-button (click)="openDialog()">OpenDialog</button>`
})
export class MyComponent {
  constructor(public dialog: MatDialog) {}

  openDialog(): void {
    const dialogRef = this.dialog.open(MyDialogContentComponent, {
      width: '250px',
      data: { title: 'Dialog Title', content: 'Dialog Content' },
    });

    dialogRef.afterClosed().subscribe(result => {
      console.log('The dialog was closed', result);
    });
  }
}
```

In this example:

The MyDialogContentComponent is the content of the dialog and includes a title, content, and a close button.

The MyComponent component uses MatDialog to open the dialog when a button is clicked.

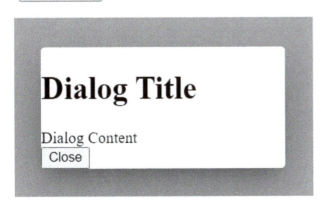

www.ingramcontent.com/pod-product-compliance
Lightning Source LLC
LaVergne TN
LVHW081530050326
832903LV00025B/1721